18 Steps to Win a Local Election

A Candidate and Volunteer Workbook

by Robert D. Butler

An **ICAN** Book

Independent Candidate Action Network

ISBN 13: 978-0-9820141-9-6
ISBN 10:0-9820141-9-8

Published in 2009 in the United States by
Adsum Press, a division of
Woolstrum Publishing House, LLC.

www.adsumpress.com
www.indyaction.org
www.governmentbasics.com

Printed in the United States of America
on acid-free paper.
All trademarks are owned by
their respective companies.

16 15 14 13 12 11 10 09 08 07 06 05 04 03 02 01

For all those who work towards greater liberty and the restoration of the Republic.

Contents

Foreword

I have run for office three times. I lost once, won twice. I have also presided as state chair of the Libertarian Party of Texas for the past six years as we have placed over three hundred candidates on the ballot. That does not make me Karl Rove or James Carville, but I have learned from my experience.

If you do not have experience running for office or working on a campaign, this book is for you. This book does have some focus on candidates running as Libertarians, but it can be applied to anyone running for office. The principles of running a good campaign are universal, but there are unique challenges when you are running against incumbents and larger political parties.

Also, do not feel that you have to do everything in this book. If you have the resources to run a complete campaign, go for it. However, for some of the smaller races, you can still win by focusing on the most important aspects conveyed in this book and tailoring the campaign to the size of your effort.

Another aspect of campaigning is that you don't have to win to win. That may be paradoxical, but there is great benefit in running for office even when the odds are against you. By running an effective campaign, you can raise issues, influence policy, and possibly be a factor in how the vote swings from one candidate to another. Playing a "kingmaker" role is a very powerful way to influence policy even if you are not the winning candidate. This book will help make the most of your efforts to be a significant player in the election.

If you are serious about influencing policy and making an impact, I highly recommend you boldly try running for office. If you run for office or want to help with a campaign, I highly recommend this book.

Yours in Liberty,

Patrick J Dixon
Libertarian Party National Committee, At-Large Member Chair,
Libertarian Party of Texas (www.LPTexas.org)

Introduction

If you go through each of the steps, you will have a solid foundation for winning a local campaign. This workbook was created to help candidates and volunteers win more elections and fight more effective campaigns. It can help you bring order to your campaigns by systematically guiding you through the campaign process.

Please keep in mind that this book was primarily written for Independents, minor party candidates, and major party reformers. For brevity, I refer to all these candidates as Independents.

The first pages of most campaign books will solemnly advise you to run as a mainstream Republican or Democrat in any partisan race. They predict that running as an Independent or (heaven forbid) a minor party candidate will be an uphill battle, and that you will probably lose. Until recently, this advice was fairly accurate. Even now, running as an Independent may be more of a liability than an asset. Nevertheless, thousands of Independent candidates now run for office every year and over eight hundred minor party officials currently sit in public office.

Countless Independents have followed the advice of these campaign books and decided to choose a party, whether it matched their philosophy of government or not. Numerous factors are taken into account in deciding whether to run as a Republican or Democrat. These factors include: the relative strength or weakness of the party in their district, the opinions of their friends and family, the financial strength of their local parties, local community issues, the support of their contributors and volunteers, and their personal beliefs.

The strength of your local party's organization is an important factor in deciding how you will run for office. Clearly, an organized party is more likely to be of assistance in your efforts to win. The local party has decades of experience. Past candidates can instruct you on the specifics of how to win in your community and help you steer clear of obstacles. They will have helpful contacts with the press, financial contributors, a list of volunteers, and perhaps a paid staff. The local party may even be able to "guarantee" your victory through its proven model of success and support among the voters.

Your friends, coworkers, and family may even be members or activists in the Republican or Democratic Parties. It is difficult to turn aside the social pressure to follow suit. Independents and minor party candidates are often ridiculed or easily dismissed as unimportant distractions from the "real race." This kind of public rejection can be hurtful and may influence your relationship with your friends and family.

Fundraising is the most important aspect of any campaign. It takes money to get a candidate's message before the public and create a professional appearance for your campaign. The major parties are very helpful in raising money. They possess long lists of local contributors who may be willing to give your campaign money simply because of your party identification. Most campaigns and the issues they champion are driven by the need to raise large sums of money. Having an established financial network takes pressure off the campaign and the candidate.

Most local political parties will be well known for championing specific local issues including taxes, bonds, bike paths, redevelopment, infrastructure, housing, and schools. You may find that a particular issue strongly resonates with your community's voters and that one of the major parties has staked a claim on that issue. This kind of party branding can often make your campaign very emotional for your neighborhood. It may even create an impossible situation for any other party's candidate to win unless he or she can successfully defuse the issue.

Sadly, personal philosophy usually takes a back seat to the candidate's desire to win office. Most candidates are able to shoe horn their personal politics into one of the major parties. They believe in cutting taxes so they become a Republican. They believe in helping the disadvantaged so they become a Democrat. They may just follow in the footsteps of their family tradition. They go along with what they've been taught in school. They may even switch parties to give themselves a better chance at success.

Why should you run as an Independent or minor party candidate? Independents are marked by a strong desire to follow their true political and personal beliefs. They often believe that government is not the most efficient method of achieving public goals. They believe that individual liberty and personal responsibility are the answers to our social ills. They disagree with Republicans when they increase spending through borrowing money. They disagree with Democrats who try to use government to solve all of our personal problems. Independents' disagreements with the major parties are so strong that they feel there is no place for them within the two-party system that governs this country.

Major Party or Minor Party?

You may consider joining one of the major parties. After all, you may be able to "change the party from within." There are certainly candidates who have taken this route. Ron Paul's Campaign for Liberty, for example, is an organization that seeks to reform the Republican Party and spread the seeds of liberty throughout our public discourse. If you do decide to run as an outsider in one of the major parties, this book will still be very helpful, especially in your primary contest.

I formed **I CAN** , the **Independent Candidate Action Network** to help liberty-minded Independents and minor party candidates raise money, build coalitions, design and create campaign materials, hire campaign staff, and offer solid strategy advice.

This book is intended to build a solid foundation for anyone interested in running for elected office. The main focus of **18 Steps to Win A Local Election** is marketing, political strategy, and campaign management. **It is important that you do not rely on this book for legal advice**, especially for financial reporting and fundraising. **Legal requirements vary from state to state and precinct to precinct, and this book is not intended to offer such counsel.** Check with your local lawyer and the Election Office before you begin your race.

There has never been a better time to be a candidate. **Go get 'em!**

Step 1:

Know My Compass

"Politics ought to be the part-time profession of every citizen who would protect the rights and privileges of free people and who would preserve what is good and fruitful in our national heritage."
 - Dwight D. Eisenhower

World's Smallest Political Quiz

Examining your own political philosophy is an important step on the campaign trail.

Answer the following questions and give yourself 20 points for every "yes," 10 points for every "maybe," and 0 points for every "no." Plot the personal and economic scores separately and see where they connect.

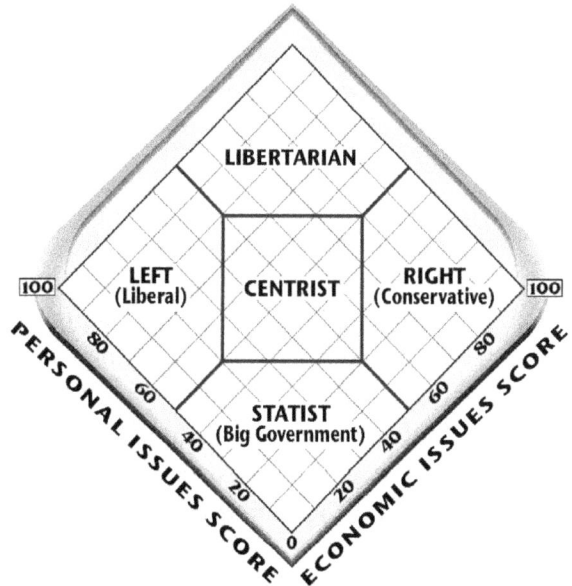

The World's Smallest Political Quiz is copyrighted and reprinted here by permission of the Advocates for Self-Government.

Personal Issues	
1. Government should not censor speech, press, media or Internet.	
2. Military service should be voluntary. There should be no draft.	
3. There should be no laws regarding sex for consenting adults.	
4. Repeal laws prohibiting adult possession and use of drugs.	
5. There should be no National ID card.	
Total =	

Economic Issues	
1. End "corporate welfare." No government handouts to business.	
2. End government barriers to international free trade.	
3. Let people control their own retirement; privatize Social Security.	
4. Replace government welfare with private charity.	
5. Cut taxes and government spending by 50% or more.	
Total =	

Successful Candidate Checklist

There are habits and characteristics shared by most successful candidates.

☐ **Confident**. A successful candidate has the confidence of knowing he/she is the best person for the job. I will be confident and explain why I am the best person for the job. A candidate may occasionally feel nervous. I will swallow that nervous energy and make it work to my advantage. A successful candidate is never too confident. I will not underestimate my opponent and the difficulty of my task is deadly.

☐ **Authentic**. Voters today crave authenticity. I will speak from my heart about things that really matter. I won't preach or intellectualize my subject matter. I may have a great speech about "Live Free or Die!" or the French economist Bastiat, but my constituents want to know that I care about their families and can fix the pothole on 12th Street.

☐ **Truthful**. The best candidates are truthful, honest, and direct. I will learn the best way to explain my position in a precise and direct manner and never lie or invent statistics. I won't hem and haw on controversial topics. I will practice my explanations and answers so that they can come through clearly. If I do not know the answer to a question, I will fully admit my lack of knowledge.

☐ **Punctual**. Good candidates are always on time or slightly early for their commitments. I will never even begin to think that my time is more valuable than my audience. When I arrive late, I've already broken my first campaign promise. My personal assistant's job is to interrupt me when necessary and keep me on schedule.

☐ **Polite**. All successful candidates are polite and civil. The easiest way to kill an angry voter is with kindness. Agree to disagree and move on. I will meet stupid people, obnoxious people, and painfully frustrating people, but they all vote.

☐ **Well-groomed**. My public appearance must convey professionalism at all times. A good rule of thumb about clothing is to imagine what everyone else will be wearing and dress slightly better. If I plan to introduce new solutions to my community, I need all the help I can get. My independence or association with a minor party has probably done some damage to my credibility already. If I do not appear to be completely professional, I will be easily written off as a kook.

☐ **Informed**. When explaining my policies, I must be ready to cite local statistics and examples of how my vision will benefit the people of my district. Always use local examples to illustrate complicated ideas. Information works two ways: I must listen to the concerns of my voters and then cite those concerns in my examples. I know I will learn much more about my district from speaking with the voters than I ever could have known before. I will be open to listen and learn.

☐ **Fundraiser**. In medium to large scale campaigns, most of the candidate's time is spent fundraising. I do not have a major party's deep pockets to tap. I will find out how much money the candidates spent to run for this office the last time. I need to raise at least as much as they did to be competitive. If I raise more money, I can either outspend them or keep it for my next race.

As a minor party or Independent candidate, I must keep in mind that most voters either have no opinion or are misinformed about my party. It is necessary for me to be ten times the candidate of my opponent. I must outshine, outwit, and outlast my opponent at every opportunity. I must be the most professional candidate my community has ever seen. In this way, I will dismiss the false rumors about my party or about Independents in general and show my true colors.

Successful Candidate Makeover Checklist

It is often difficult for candidates to understand the importance of their appearance or accept any professional assistance in this regard.

I will check off each item as I address it with my campaign staff. I will make sure that at least one of my staff or volunteers has some experience with fashion and personal care. Keep in mind, your campaign wardrobe needs to be separate and distinct from your personal clothing.

☐ One or two professional, well-tailored business suits in the latest style (for men or women).

☐ A few sets of new business casual button-down shirts and pants or the female equivalent to wear when I am outdoors. (The wrinkle-free variety is recommended for shirts and pants.)

☐ Professional and comfortable shoes that are designed to keep a high shine without polishing.

☐ Facial hair for men must be properly trimmed. (Ask for others' opinions.)

☐ Men and women should update their hair styles. Women also need to update their make-up styles. (Ask for opinions.)

☐ Remember that this is only to freshen your look. It is important for you to be authentic and to be the best you that you can be.

NOTES:

18 Steps to Win a Local Election

Step 2:

Know My Political Organizations

"If you know neither the enemy nor yourself, you will succumb in every battle."- Sun Tzu

Exercise 1: Match the national organization with its description. Write the letter in the space provided.

1. Green Party   _____
2. State Policy Network   _____
3. Campaign for Liberty   _____
4. CATO Institute   _____
5. Libertarian Party   _____
6. National Center for Constitutional Studies   _____
7. Constitution Party   _____
8. I CAN Independent Candidate Action Network   _____
9. League of Women's Voters   _____

a. An educational organization founded by Cleon Skousen, famous for books: *5,000 Year Leap* and *Making of America*.

b. A nonpartisan political organization, encourages informed and active participation in government through education and advocacy.

c. The only group in the country dedicated solely to improving the practical effectiveness of independent, non-profit, market-oriented, state-based think tanks.

d. A Christian conservative political party that promotes American sovereignty and conservative moral and economic values.

e. A network of state parties that advocate environmental policies and social equality.

f. Ron Paul's non-profit organization to promote American sovereignty, free market economics, a return to the gold standard, and the original intent of the Constitution.

g. Founded in 1977 by Edward H. Crane to increase the understanding of public policies based on the principles of limited government, free markets, individual liberty, and peace.

h. A political party that advocates individual liberty, personal responseability, and free market economics with over six hundred elected officials.

i. A peer-to-peer network of voters, volunteers, candidates, and contributors who work together to promote Independent and minor party campaigns.

Exercise 2: Know My Local Political Organizations

1. Political Parties in My State

Constitution Party

Chair's Name	Phone	Email	Mailing Address

Democratic Party

Chair's Name	Phone	Email	Mailing Address

Green Party

Chair's Name	Phone	Email	Mailing Address

Libertarian Party

Chair's Name	Phone	Email	Mailing Address

Republican Party

Chair's Name	Phone	Email	Mailing Address

2. Other Organizations in My State

Organization:

Chair's Name	Phone	Email	Mailing Address

Organization:

Chair's Name	Phone	Email	Mailing Address

Organization:

Chair's Name	Phone	Email	Mailing Address

3. Political Parties in My County

Constitution Party
Chair's Name | Phone | Email | Mailing Address

Democratic Party
Chair's Name | Phone | Email | Mailing Address

Green Party
Chair's Name | Phone | Email | Mailing Address

Libertarian Party
Chair's Name | Phone | Email | Mailing Address

Republican Party
Chair's Name | Phone | Email | Mailing Address

4. Other Organizations in My County

Organization:
Chair's Name | Phone | Email | Mailing Address

Organization:
Chair's Name | Phone | Email | Mailing Address

Organization:
Chair's Name | Phone | Email | Mailing Address

5. Political Parties in My City or Subdivision

Constitution Party

Chair's Name	Phone	Email	Mailing Address

Democratic Party

Chair's Name	Phone	Email	Mailing Address

Green Party

Chair's Name	Phone	Email	Mailing Address

Libertarian Party

Chair's Name	Phone	Email	Mailing Address

Republican Party

Chair's Name	Phone	Email	Mailing Address

6. Other Organizations in My City or Subdivision

Organization:

Chair's Name	Phone	Email	Mailing Address

Organization:

Chair's Name	Phone	Email	Mailing Address

Organization:

Chair's Name	Phone	Email	Mailing Address

7. Political Parties in My Precint

Constitution Party

Chair's Name	Phone	Email	Mailing Address

Democratic Party

Chair's Name	Phone	Email	Mailing Address

Green Party

Chair's Name	Phone	Email	Mailing Address

Libertarian Party

Chair's Name	Phone	Email	Mailing Address

Republican Party

Chair's Name	Phone	Email	Mailing Address

8. Other Organizations in My Precinct

Organization:

Chair's Name	Phone	Email	Mailing Address

Organization:

Chair's Name	Phone	Email	Mailing Address

Organization:

Chair's Name	Phone	Email	Mailing Address

NOTES:

❧ Step 3: ❧

Prepare for Winning Office

The voters are looking for a competent person to lead their community.

If you are planning to run for political office, take leadership roles in the community. List them below.

Goals for this year:

My Community Groups

Organization:

Name	Phone	Email	Mailing Address

Organization:

Name	Phone	Email	Mailing Address

Organization:

Name	Phone	Email	Mailing Address

Hot Issues in My Community

1.

2.

3.

My Personal, Educational, and Professional Qualifications for Office

1.

2.

3.

I can build my qualifications in the next 12 months by:

Studying: _____

Joining: _____

**Doing
research on:** _____

Meeting: _____

Reading: _____

**Practicing
public
speaking by:** _____

NOTES:

Step 4:

Pick the Right Race at the Right Time

Make a list of the current office holders who represent your county. Find out how much money they spent in their most recent elections, how many votes were cast in their elections, and how many registered voters and households were in their districts. Complete this chart to estimate the level of difficulty.

Office	Name	Money Spent	Votes Cast	Reg. Voters	Households	Level of Difficulty

Office	Name	Money Spent	Votes Cast	Reg. Voters	Households	Level of Difficulty

Exercise 1: Harford county is an exurban/rural county north of Baltimore, Maryland. The county executive, the county president, and the sheriff are at-large seats.

Here is the map of county council seats elected by district. Plot the results of this election on the Harford County Council Map. Look for partisan voting trends throughout the county.

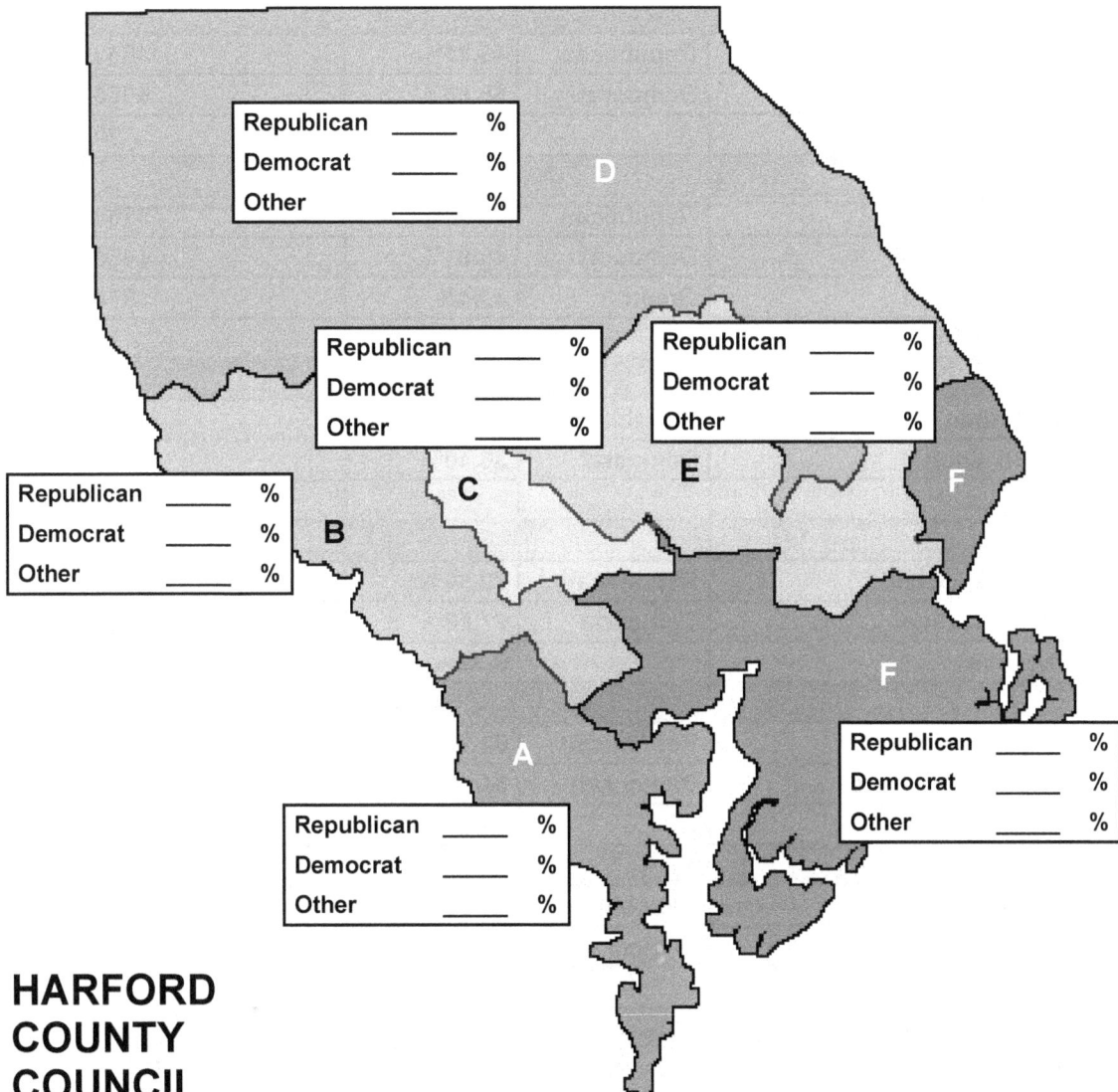

D

Republican	_____	%
Democrat	_____	%
Other	_____	%

C

Republican	_____	%
Democrat	_____	%
Other	_____	%

E

Republican	_____	%
Democrat	_____	%
Other	_____	%

B

Republican	_____	%
Democrat	_____	%
Other	_____	%

F

Republican	_____	%
Democrat	_____	%
Other	_____	%

A

Republican	_____	%
Democrat	_____	%
Other	_____	%

HARFORD COUNTY COUNCIL

Map taken from Harford County government, Hardford County, Maryland.

Office/Name	Party	Percentage	Totals
COUNTY EXECUTIVE			Total Votes 88662
Craig, David	Republican	52.02%	46121
Helton, Ann	Democrat	47.87%	42442
Write-in		0.11%	99
PRES COUNTY COUNCIL			Total Votes 87409
Boniface, Billy	Republican	66.06%	57743
White, Charles	Democrat	33.85%	29591
Write-in		0.09%	75
COUNTY COUNCIL A			Total Votes 10768
Biggs, Christopher	Republican	43.21%	4653
Guthrie, Dion	Democrat	56.60%	6095
Write-in		0.19%	20
COUNTY COUNCIL B			Total Votes 16206
Chenowith, Roni	Republican	50.39%	8166
Twanmoh, Val	Democrat	46.01%	7456
Bittner, Brian	Green	3.54%	574
Write-in Votes		0.06%	10
COUNTY COUNCIL C			Total Votes 17384
McMahan, James	Republican	63.47%	11034
Ward, Joan	Democrat	36.40%	6328
Write-in		0.13%	22
COUNTY COUNCIL D			Total Votes 15725
Shrodes, Chad	Republican	72.50%	11400
Cox, Terence	Democrat	27.18%	4274
Write-in		0.32%	51
COUNTY COUNCIL E			Total Votes 14837
Slutzky, Richard	Republican	62.78%	9314
Wheeler, Leonard	Democrat	37.17%	5515
Write-in		0.05%	8
COUNTY COUNCIL F			Total Votes 12323
Correri, John P	Republican	39.58%	4877
Lisanti, Mary Ann	Democrat	60.32%	7433
Write-in		0.11%	13
SHERIFF			Total Votes 86757
Cochran, Norm	Republican	42.42%	36799
Bane, Jesse	Democrat	57.32%	49729
Write-in		0.26%	229

Targeting Questions

1. After analyzing the data, what is the average vote for Republicans and Democrats countywide?

_____

_____

2. Who had a weak performance? Who had a strong performance? Who is vulnerable? (It's important to remember that vulnerable politicians are usually more persuadable in office.)

_____

_____

_____

3. If I were in charge of a countywide pro-liberty organization, which of these office holders would I try to recruit to my team? Who would I target for replacement?

_____

_____

_____

4. Who would I like to run against? Why? And under which party banner?

_____

_____

_____

5. Harford county has two distinct sections. Divide this map into Republican and Democratic areas based on the numbers.

6. Make an educated guess and divide the county into rural, suburb, and urban areas.

7. Can I guess the average educational levels? Income? Racial make-up? How about the percentage of home owners vs. renters?

Exercise 2: Checking the US Census

Example 1: Exurban/Rural Counties: High profile, high budget campaigns can afford to spend hundreds of thousands of dollars on targeting and micro-targeting, but we can get a lot of free data from the U.S. Census Bureau. All of the following data was found at http://factfinder.census.gov. How does this data correlate with the election numbers?

Harford County College Graduates

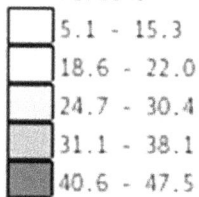

Data Classes

Percent

	5.1 - 15.3
	18.6 - 22.0
	24.7 - 30.4
	31.1 - 38.1
	40.6 - 47.5

Features

/\/ Major Road

Street

Stream/Waterbody

/\/ Stream/Waterbody

Items in gray text
are not visible
at this zoom level

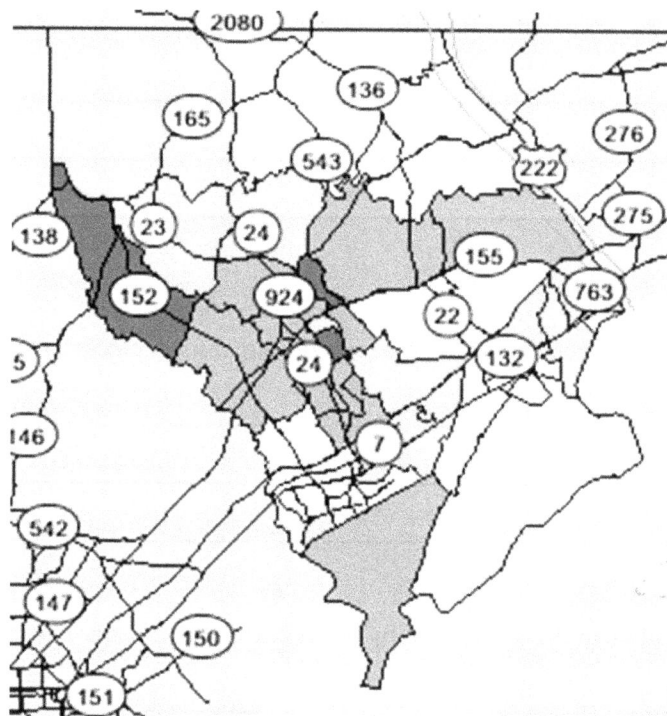

Harford County Median Family Income

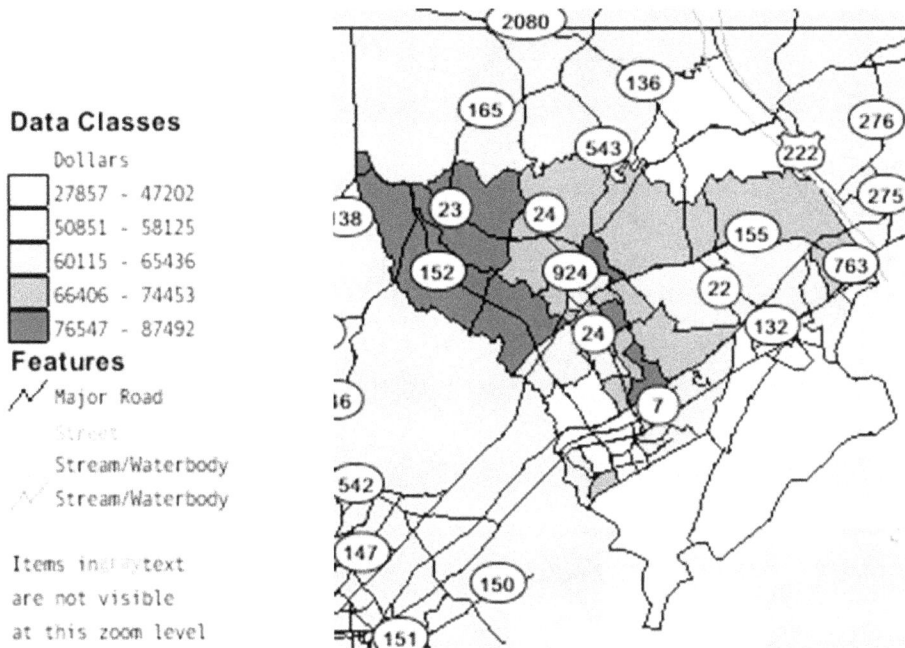

Data Classes

Dollars
- 27857 - 47202
- 50851 - 58125
- 60115 - 65436
- 66406 - 74453
- 76547 - 87492

Features
- Major Road
- Street
- Stream/Waterbody
- Stream/Waterbody

Items in graytext
are not visible
at this zoom level

Harford County Residents of African Descent

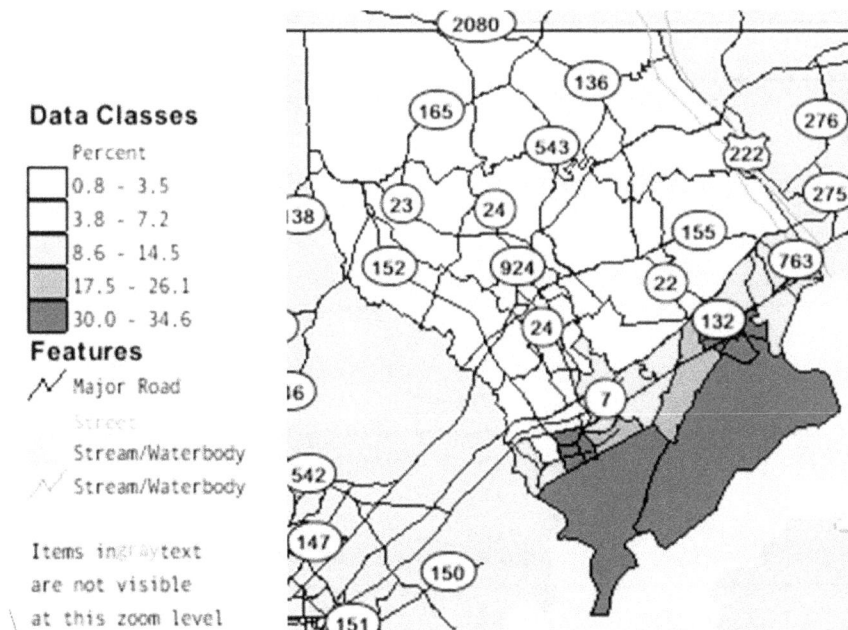

Data Classes

Percent
- 0.8 - 3.5
- 3.8 - 7.2
- 8.6 - 14.5
- 17.5 - 26.1
- 30.0 - 34.6

Features
- Major Road
- Street
- Stream/Waterbody
- Stream/Waterbody

Items in graytext
are not visible
at this zoom level

Harford County Renter Occupied Housing Units

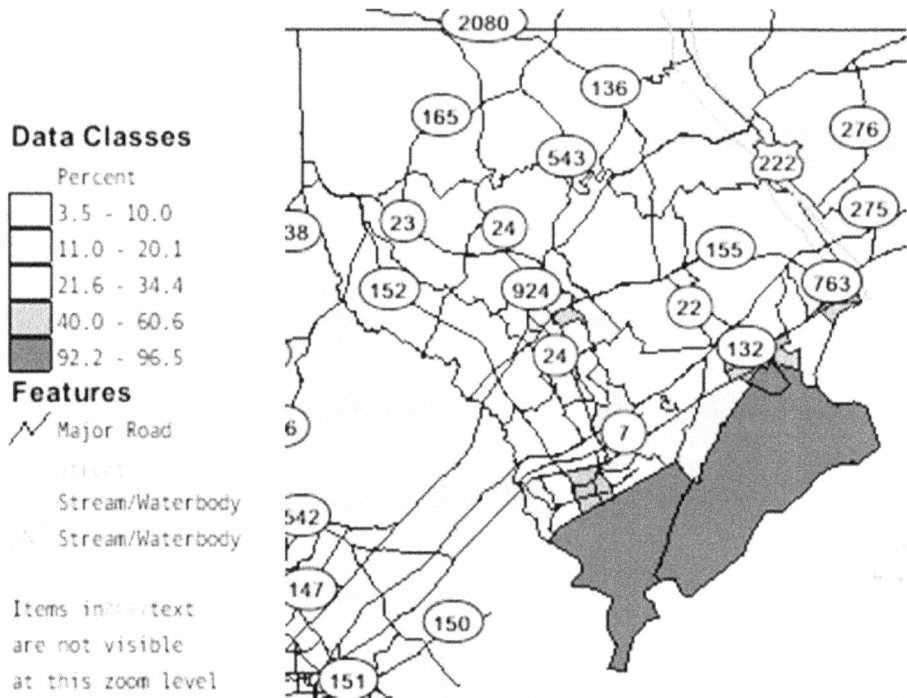

Data Classes

Percent

☐	3.5 - 10.0
☐	11.0 - 20.1
☐	21.6 - 34.4
▨	40.0 - 60.6
▦	92.2 - 96.5

Features

⟋ Major Road

Street

Stream/Waterbody

⟋ Stream/Waterbody

Items in text
are not visible
at this zoom level

Carefully compare and examine these demographic maps with the election results map.
Are there any interesting trends?

_____

_____

Example 2: Political Maps of the Big Cities: Indianapolis clearly demonstrates the classic sunny-side up, fried egg shape of a modern American city. A renewed urban center surrounded by the first ring of poor suburbs and the second ring of wealthier suburbs and rapidly expanding exurbs.

Indianapolis College Graduates

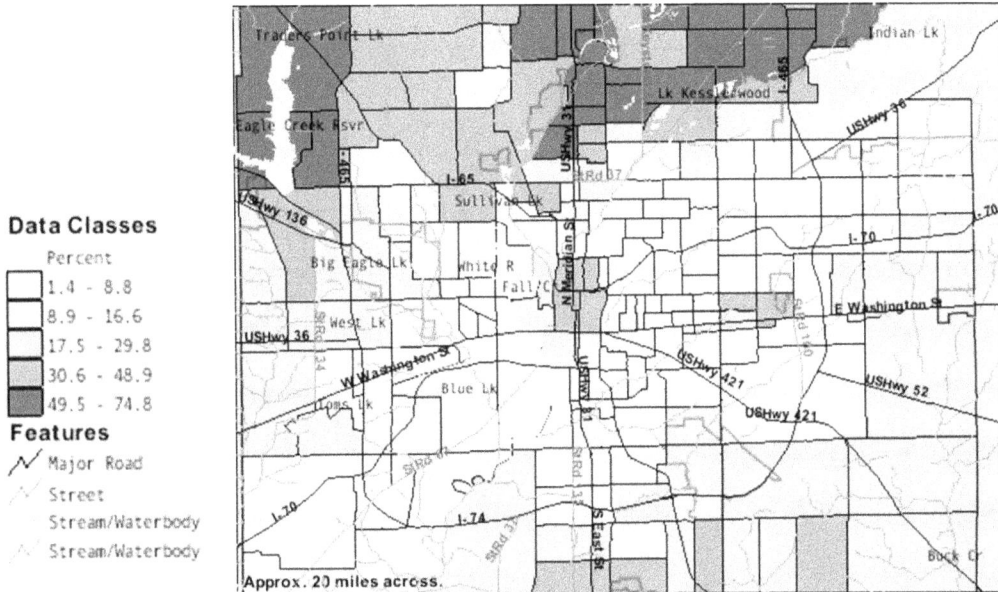

Data Classes
Percent
1.4 - 8.8
8.9 - 16.6
17.5 - 29.8
30.6 - 48.9
49.5 - 74.8
Features
Major Road
Street
Stream/Waterbody
Stream/Waterbody
Approx. 20 miles across.

The following maps were taken from the Marion County government, Marion County, Indiana.

Indianapolis Median Family Income

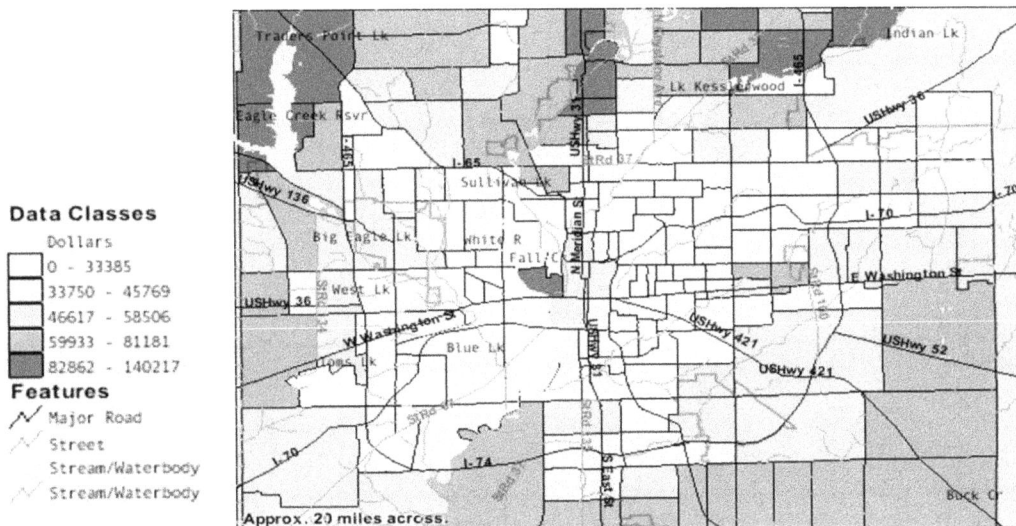

Data Classes
Dollars
0 - 33385
33750 - 45769
46617 - 58506
59933 - 81181
82862 - 140217
Features
Major Road
Street
Stream/Waterbody
Stream/Waterbody
Approx. 20 miles across.

Indianapolis Renter Occupied Housing Units

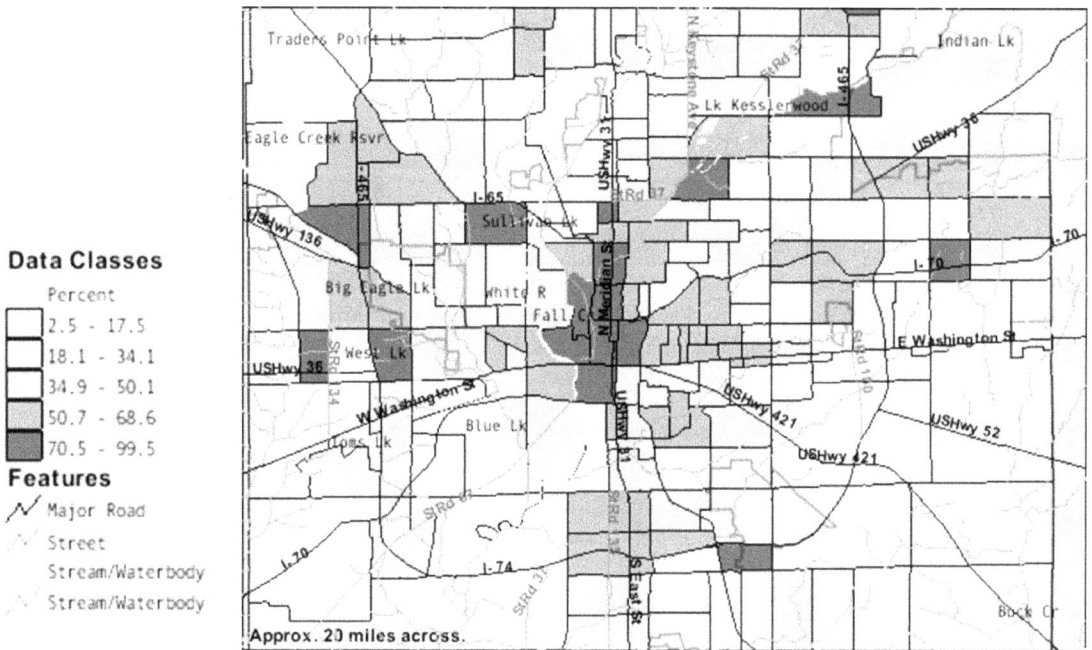

Data Classes

Percent

- 2.5 - 17.5
- 18.1 - 34.1
- 34.9 - 50.1
- 50.7 - 68.6
- 70.5 - 99.5

Features

- Major Road
- Street
- Stream/Waterbody
- Stream/Waterbody

Approx. 20 miles across.

Residents of African Descent

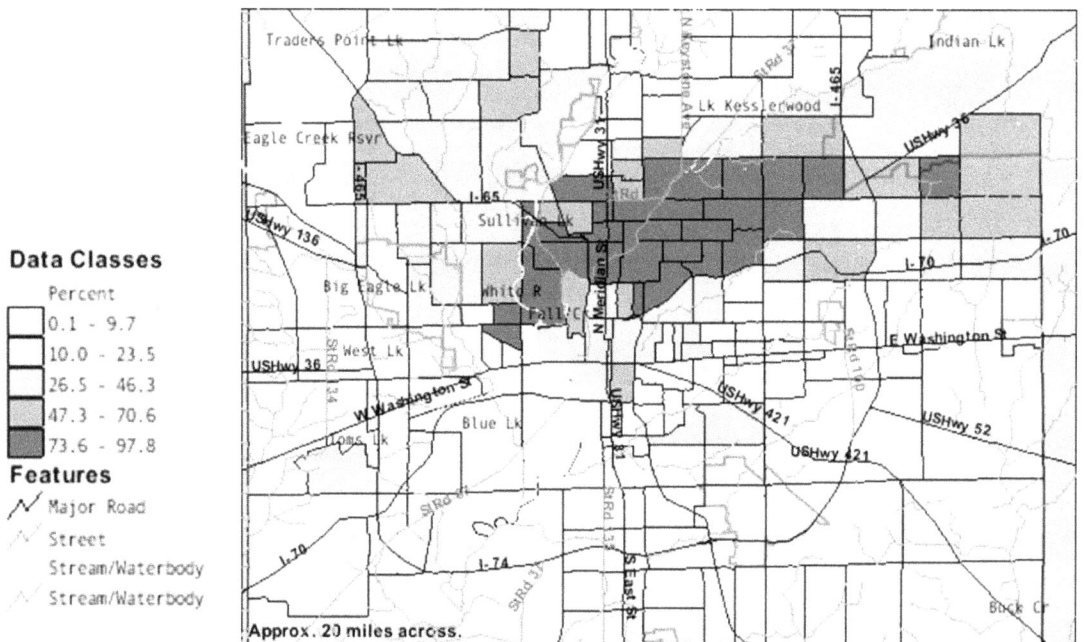

Data Classes

Percent

- 0.1 - 9.7
- 10.0 - 23.5
- 26.5 - 46.3
- 47.3 - 70.6
- 73.6 - 97.8

Features

- Major Road
- Street
- Stream/Waterbody
- Stream/Waterbody

Approx. 20 miles across.

What can you deduce about city politics in Indianapolis from these maps?

_____

_____

Indianapolis State Representative Race

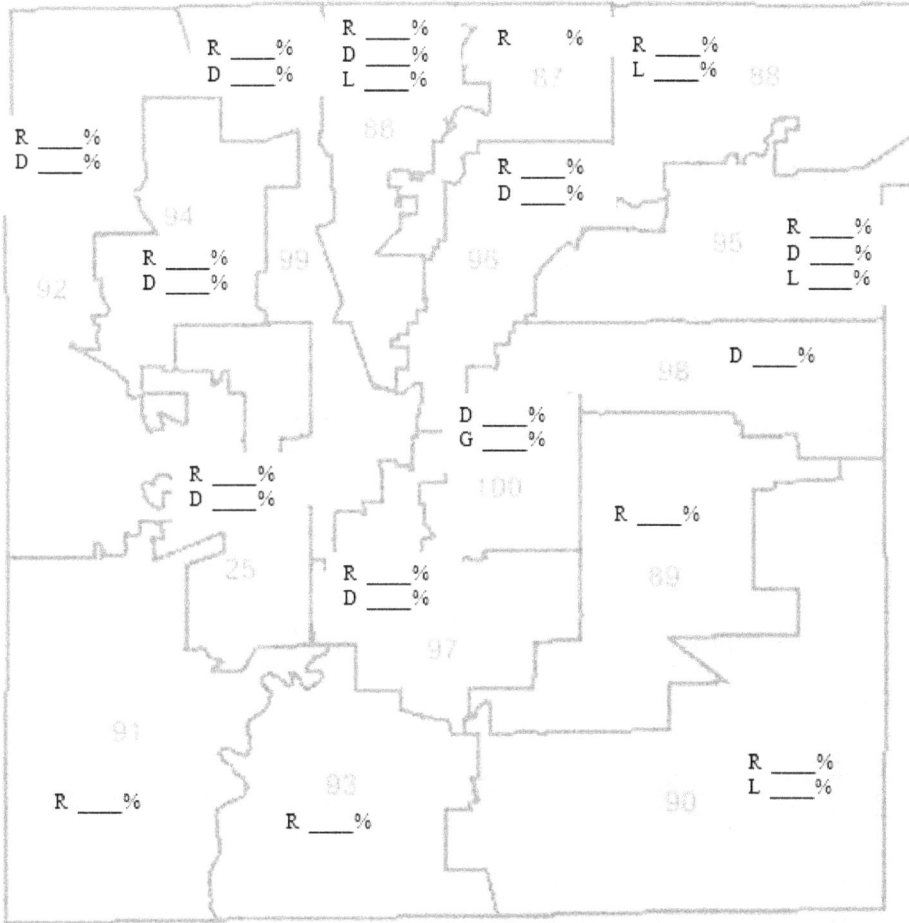

Here is a map of the state representatives' districts in Indianapolis. Can you make an educated guess about where each party will do well based on the demographic maps shown on the previous pages?

Plot the election results into this map to see if your predictions prove to be accurate. What trends are evident in Indianapolis?

_____

_____

Which district would you like to run in? Why?

_____

District	Candidate	Votes	Percent
District 25	Bardon, Jeb (Democratic)	8320	66%
	Foreman, Dennis K. (Republican)	4242	34%
District 86	Orentlicher, David (Democratic)	13058	58%
	Goldstein, Sam (Libertarian)	461	2%
	Large, Morton R. (Republican)	8994	40%
District 87	Noe, Cynthia Jean (Republican)	10553	33.5%
District 88	Gordon, Aaron C. (Libertarian)	1821	6%
	Bosma, Brian C. (Republican)	19109	60.5%
District 89	Buell, Lawrence L. (Republican)	15391	100%
District 90	Brenton, Dorn (Libertarian)	1779	8%
	Murphy, Michael B. (Republican)	21389	92%
District 91	Behning, Robert W. (Republican)	7279	100%
District 92	Swinford Jr., Allen (Democratic)	9488	37%
	Hinkle, Phillip D. (Republican)	16158	63%
District 93	Frizzell, David Nason (Republican)	12905	100%
District 94	Mays, Carolene (Democratic)	14827	71%
	Wheeler, Brent (Libertarian)	381	2%
	Brinkman, Shane (Republican)	5629	27%
District 95	Dickinson, Mae (Democratic)	14875	71%
	Barnes, Eric J. (Libertarian)	474	2%
	Black, Lyman Tex (Republican)	5555	27%
District 96	Porter, Gregory W. (Democratic)	15774	69%
	Jessen, Brian M. (Republican)	7009	31%
District 97	Mahern, Edmund M. (Democratic)	7705	54%
	Butler, Roxanne (Republican)	6646	46%
District 98	Crawford, William A. (Democratic)	15143	100%
District 99	Summers, Vanessa J. (Democratic)	14909	70%
	Davies, Jeffrey R. (Republican)	6383	30%
District 100	Day, John J. (Democratic)	8739	99.9%
	Hayes, Bethany M (W/I(Green))	5	0.1%

Exercise 3: Prioritize My Pricincts

☐ Find the maps and the election results from at least the last eight years.

☐ Narrow down to the precinct level maps and results. Map out all the various elections held in the precincts for the last eight years.

☐ Determine which race would be the easiest to run in politically.

☐ Determine which precincts are favorable to your party and message, swing precincts, and unfavorable precincts.

☐ Determine which precincts you need to win and how many votes you can reasonably expect to receive from each precinct to top fifty percent.

In each precinct, estimate the total votes that will be cast and calculate my minimum number to top fifty percent, the expected total, and the stretch goal total. These numbers can help you decide a range of issues, including where to place yard signs, walk door-to-door, and send mailings. The success of your entire campaign depends on these numbers.

Precinct Number	Total Votes	My Minimum Vote Total	My Expected Vote Total	My Stretch Goal Total

NOTES:

18 Steps to Win a Local Election

Step 5:

Speak with My Priority Contacts

"There is no surer tie between friends than when they are united in their objectives and wishes."
                                                    -Marcus Tullius Cicero

Make a list of the twenty-five most important people to the success of your campaign. They will be top contributors and/or work the most volunteer hours. Contact them before the campaign officially starts to win their support. Be open to their suggestions about which office to pursue and show them the information gathered in the previous exercise.

Name	Address	Phone	Email	Notes

Name	Address	Phone	Email	Notes

Notes on results:

NOTES:

Step 6:

Appoint My Campaign Committee

By this time, you have notified all your contacts that you are planning to run for office. Now start your official campaign committee. Requirements for campaign committees vary. Be sure to comply with the local laws. In most states, the treasurer is legally responsible for following all campaign finance laws and filing the related documentation by certain deadlines. Campaign committees are usually honorific and not real working committees, but that decision is yours.

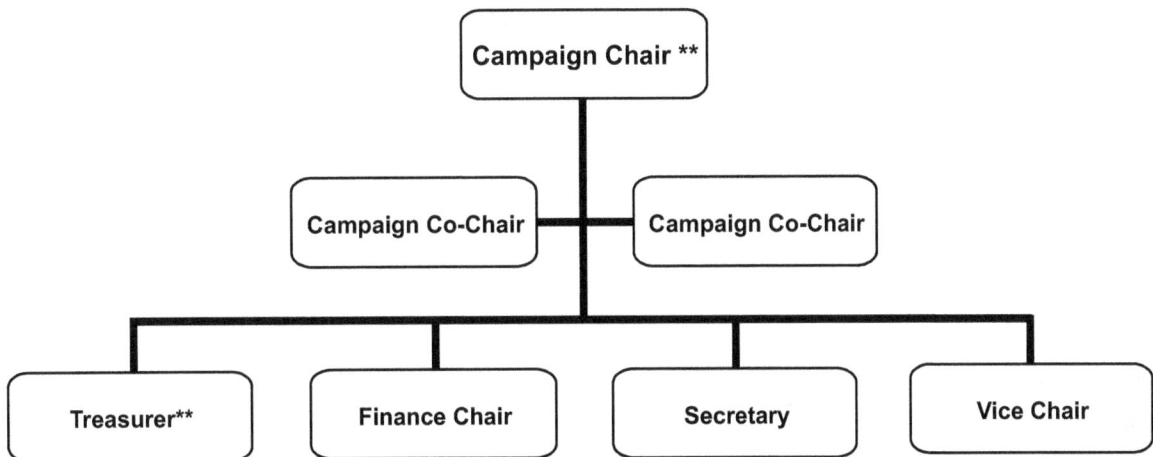

```
                    ┌──────────────────────┐
                    │  Campaign Chair **    │
                    └──────────────────────┘
                               │
          ┌────────────────────┼────────────────────┐
          │                                         │
┌──────────────────┐                    ┌──────────────────┐
│ Campaign Co-Chair│                    │ Campaign Co-Chair│
└──────────────────┘                    └──────────────────┘
          │
┌──────────┬──────────────┬──────────────┬──────────────┐
│          │              │              │              │
┌────────────┐ ┌────────────┐ ┌────────────┐ ┌────────────┐
│ Treasurer**│ │Finance Chair│ │ Secretary │ │ Vice Chair │
└────────────┘ └────────────┘ └────────────┘ └────────────┘
```

** Often the only legally required positions, check with the local Election Office

My Campaign Committee

Chair
Name   Phone   Email   Mailing Address

Co-Chair (if I have interested VIP's)
Name   Phone   Email   Mailing Address

Co-Chair (if I have interested VIP's)
Name   Phone   Email   Mailing Address

Vice Chair
Name   Phone   Email   Mailing Address

Finance Chair
Name   Phone   Email   Mailing Address

Treasurer
Name   Phone   Email   Mailing Address

Secretary
Name   Phone   Email   Mailing Address

Notes on results:

NOTES:

Step 7:

Hire My Campaign Staff

During this final phase of planning, locate and hire a campaign staff. Once you have decided upon a campaign manager, both of you can discuss the rest of the staff. In small campaigns, everyone may be a volunteer, and there may be one person filling several (or all) the job titles. It is still important to know what those titles are and what duties each is expected to perform. It is also important to treat the campaign as a business with hiring and dismissal (of paid or unpaid staff) based on performance.

This is a sample chart. More positions could be created.

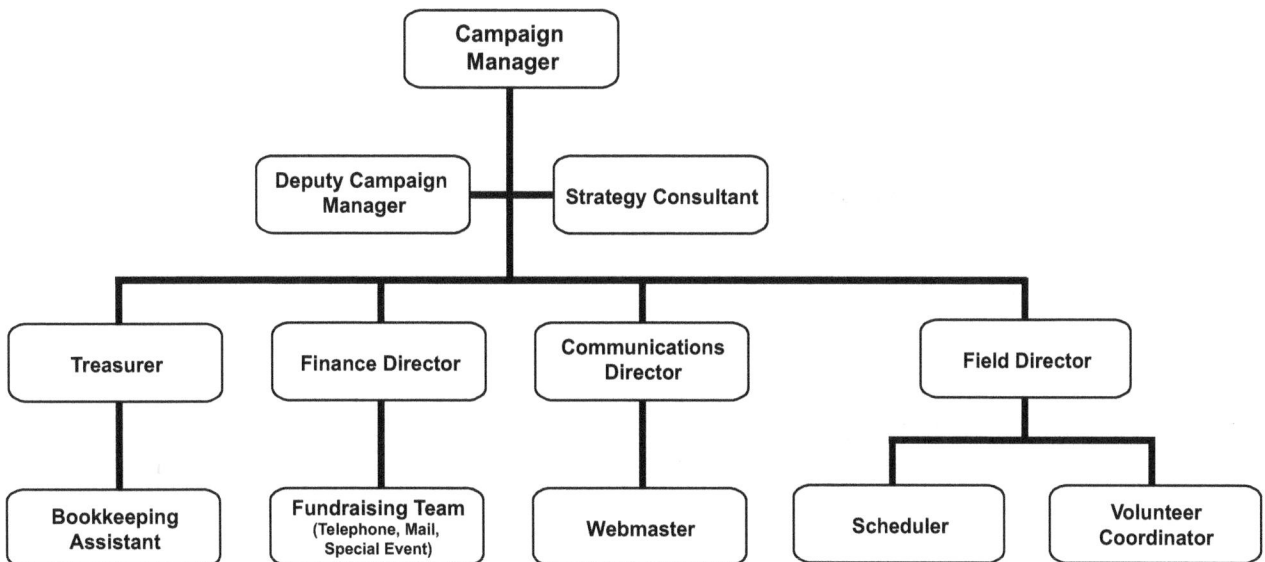

```
                          ┌──────────────┐
                          │   Campaign   │
                          │   Manager    │
                          └──────────────┘
         ┌──────────────────┐      ┌──────────────────┐
         │ Deputy Campaign  │      │ Strategy         │
         │ Manager          │      │ Consultant       │
         └──────────────────┘      └──────────────────┘

  ┌───────────┐  ┌───────────────┐  ┌───────────────┐  ┌───────────────┐
  │ Treasurer │  │Finance Director│  │Communications │  │Field Director │
  │           │  │               │  │Director       │  │               │
  └───────────┘  └───────────────┘  └───────────────┘  └───────────────┘
  ┌───────────┐  ┌───────────────┐  ┌───────────────┐  ┌──────────┐ ┌──────────────┐
  │Bookkeeping│  │Fundraising Team│  │  Webmaster    │  │Scheduler │ │  Volunteer   │
  │Assistant  │  │(Telephone,Mail,│  │               │  │          │ │ Coordinator  │
  │           │  │ Special Event) │  │               │  │          │ │              │
  └───────────┘  └───────────────┘  └───────────────┘  └──────────┘ └──────────────┘
```

My Campaign Staff

Campaign Manager

Name   Phone   Email   Mailing Address

Deputy Campaign Manager

Name   Phone   Email   Mailing Address

Strategy Consultant

Name   Phone   Email   Mailing Address

Communications Director

Name   Phone   Email   Mailing Address

Field Director

Name   Phone   Email   Mailing Address

Scheduler

Name   Phone   Email   Mailing Address

Webmaster

Name   Phone   Email   Mailing Address

Volunteer Coordinator

Name   Phone   Email   Mailing Address

Volunteer Checklist

- ☐ I will take a volunteer sign-up sheet everywhere.

- ☐ I will keep accurate records of volunteer contact information.

- ☐ I will give volunteers something to do as soon as they offer to help.

- ☐ I will explain why their task is important to the campaign.

- ☐ I will pay attention to each individual's strengths and weaknesses and assign tasks accordingly. I will move the good ones into staff positions.

- ☐ I will schedule fifty percent more volunteers than needed for any project.

- ☐ I will help volunteers to stay motivated by sharing good news and making them feel important. I will keep them up to date as much as possible. I will make sure they know they are an important part of the campaign.

- ☐ I will not lose my temper with volunteers, especially when they show up late or fail to attend at all.

- ☐ I will not criticize the staff, other volunteers, or the candidate in front of them.

- ☐ I will not allow volunteers to use the campaign for their own purposes. They can't leave non-campaign materials around headquarters or use the campaign to advocate other groups or causes.

- ☐ Volunteers need to be reasonably friendly and easy-going; I will not allow hard-line activists to turn off the voters.

- ☐ I will have a system to allow volunteers to submit their suggestions but will not let them disrupt the campaign plan.

Campaign Headquarters Checklist

Look for a free (donated) or reasonably priced office for rent with as many of these characteristics as possible. *Communication is the single most important purpose of a political campaign and is a high priority when choosing an office.

☐ Located in a precinct I'm running in

☐ Has electricity, running water, and bathroom(s)

☐ Has Internet access and adequate telephone and/or cable connections*

☐ Has multiple phone lines for voice, Internet, and fax*

☐ Clean and neat

☐ Has large empty space for volunteers, storage of materials, signs

☐ Has a private room with a door when privacy is needed

☐ Has a secure lock and alarm system

☐ Has a secure and locked mailbox

☐ Handicap accessible and easy to enter with large/heavy boxes

☐ Owner is willing to accept short-term lease agreement

Other Requirements for My Campaign Headquarters

☐ _____

☐ _____

☐ _____

NOTES:

Step 8:

Identify My Spending Priorities

A common mistake in many small and micro-campaigns is to spend campaign money too early on unnecessary items. Examine some "what if" scenarios. What if I only raise $5,000 from my immediate friends and family and nothing else comes in? What if I raise $10k, $20k, $30k? How should that money be spent and in what order? In some ways, it can be easier to budget for large campaigns with their larger margin for error, but if I only have $3,000 in a micro-campaign, I want to be sure it's spent properly. Also check the spending reports of previous candidates for this race to see what worked well for them. Price everything out in advance. These priorities also serve as great fundraising goals.

My First $1,000

1. _____   3. _____

2. _____   4. _____

My First $5,000

1. _____   3. _____

2. _____   4. _____

My Second $5,000

1. _____   3. _____

2. _____   4. _____

Anything Over $10,000

1. _____   4. _____

2. _____   5. _____

3. _____   6. _____

NOTES:

18 Steps to Win a Local Election

Step 9:

Create My Budget

Check the amount of money spent by the previous winner for this race. The low budget will be half of the expenses of the previous winner of this office. The medium budget will be 10% more than previous winner. The high budget will be double the previous winner's expenses.

		Low	Medium	High
Advertising	Total			
	Bulk Mail Permit			
	Bulk Rate Postage			
	Business Cards			
	Door Hangers			
	Postcards			
	Promotional Give-aways			
	Radio Ads ($/spot x frequency x days)			
	Television Ads (spot x frequency x days)			
	Website			
Fundraising	Total			
	Event Expenses			
	First-class Postage			
	Stationary (Follow up letter and pledge cards)			
	Thank-you Cards/Envelopes			

		Low	Medium	High
Office	Total			
(Try to borrow office cable, phone, and internet equipment)	Computers			
	Fax Machine			
	Paper			
	Printer			
	Rent			
Staff	Total			
(Salary; Expenses)	Campaign Manager			
	Communications Director			
	Deputy Campaign Manager			
	Field Director			
	Finance Chair			
	Scheduler			
	Volunteer Coordinator			
	Webmaster			
Travel	Total			
	Car Mileage			
	Gasoline			
	Parking Fees			
Other	Total			

Ask yourself...

What would I cut back? What would I buy first? What would I add if I raise more money?

_____

_____

What if I can borrow a free office? These are the questions I should answer before the race begins.

_____

_____

_____

_____

_____

_____

Compare your budget with those of previous candidates for this office, especially the winners. Where did they focus their money? Should you follow their example?

_____

_____

_____

_____

_____

NOTES:

❧ Step 10: ❧

Plan My Fundraising Income

The Fundraising Checklist

There are many, many ways to raise money, and your campaign should be as creative as possible. Here's a list of the most common ways, but don't let this list limit your creativity.

☐ I put the *Fun* in *Fun*draising.

☐ I have opened my campaign with the local elections office and got a bank account BEFORE raising or spending any campaign money (in most states).

☐ Pledge Cards
- Professional looking
- Made on cardstock
- Easy to photocopy in color or black ink
- Blank spaces for all the data required by the elections office
- A space for credit card info
- My campaign address in case it's being mailed

☐ I meet with family and friends privately to ask for contributions and volunteer time.

☐ I obtain telephone and mailing lists and make the calls.
- Clubs, churches, and other affiliated organizations
- Focus most efforts on like-minded political groups
- Some of these groups can give lists for free, some may charge, and some may not be permitted.

☐ I follow up telephone conversations with a prompt letter, return envelope, and pledge card. I thank the contributor for their pledge.

☐ Bulk fundraising mailers: I will target local political activists and minor party members. I will not randomly send letters to potential voters to solicit money.

☐ The campaign website must have a secure contributions page. I will make sure to collect all the data needed for reporting requirements.

☐ I have added an online store. There are many turnkey online stores like Cafepress.

☐ I will organize fundraising events.
  • Dinner or cocktail parties
  • Outdoor barbecues
  • Chili cook-off's: I will ask for people to compete (this is nice because they cook all their own food)
  • Breakfasts are popular since pancakes are inexpensive
  • Morning or evening coffees

☐ The crucial aspect of a fundraising event at the local level is that it must not cost the campaign much money. In fact, I will find people who are willing to host the event and pay for the food.

☐ Local fundraising events often happen in people's homes.

☐ The candidate should never have a fundraiser in his/her own home. It can be a lose-lose proposition. If the candidate's home is too nice, people might think twice about my fundraising need. If the home is too shabby, people might think it isn't good enough.

☐ I plan little opportunities where people can spend additional money.
  • Find a volunteer artist to come and draw sketches of your guests
  • Hold a silent auction.
  • Hold a real auction if you know a great smooth talker
I will make sure to check the laws in my state, especially if I plan any type of gambling, bingo, or raffles that may be illegal.

☐ I ask guests for money at least three times during my fundraising event. The first ask might be the admission fee. The second ask is the silent auction. The third ask might be a campaign progress report from the manager. An additional ask could be the candidate making a personal appeal.

☐ I thank my contributors. Everyone who volunteers and contributes to the campaign should get a thank you note. Local campaigns are usually small enough that each person should also get a personal phone call from the candidate.

☐ I plan my fundraising. Just as you plan expenses, you need to plan your income from fundraising. I will calculate how much money I will need for the entire campaign and how much I will need to raise each day, each week, and each month to achieve that goal.

☐ I do not stop fundraising just because I haven't met the goal. I can either spend more money on advertising, or save it for my next run for office. Nothing impresses and discourages future opponents like the size of a campaign war chest.

Fundraising Income Sources	Planned	Received
Friends and Family (Personal Visits)		
Business Associates, Clients, Vendors		
Fellow Members of Organizations		
Fundraising Event #1		
Fundraising Event #2		
Fundraising Event # 3		
Website		
Other		
Other		
Other		

NOTES:

❧ Step 11: ❧

Control My Campaign Expenses

It is vital that the top staff—candidate, campaign manager, and treasurer—understand the campaign expense reporting requirements for your race.

☐ I account for every expense with a receipt. (Check the local rules.)

☐ If someone spends money on the campaign and cannot produce a receipt, I congratulate and thank them for their contribution but do not reimburse them. (Some states exclude this requirement for small items.)

☐ Campaign checks should require two signatures if permitted.

☐ It's also a good idea to place a "void after 30 days" message on each check.

☐ My staff should meet once per week to discuss campaign expenses, fundraising locations, and how much cash is on hand.

☐ The budget should be compared to actual expenses and adjusted. Checks can be signed, bills paid, and invoices reviewed at this meeting.

☐ I reaffirm priorities in light of fundraising results. I discuss the ups and downs of the previous week and set goals for the next week.

NOTES:

18 Steps to Win a Local Election

Step 12:

Be the Answer
by Framing the Question

The winning candidate has the most compelling story told to the most voters. You are a unique individual with very specific experiences and characteristics that make you a special candidate for public office. The job of your campaign is to frame a question in the public's mind. The candidate's job is to be the answer to that question. So when designing a campaign message and theme, it's a bit like the popular game show *Jeopardy!*. We know the answer is me, but we need to properly frame the question.

To what question am I the best and most unique answer in this race?

_____

_____

How am I the best answer to the question framed above?

_____

_____

Exercise 1: Issues in My Community

1. Name three important economic issues in my local community.
   1. _____
   2. _____
   3. _____

2. Name three important social issues in my local community.
   1. _____
   2. _____
   3. _____

3. Name three important political issues in my local community.
   1. _____
   2. _____
   3. _____

From these nine local issues, am I the best candidate to provide a unique solution to any of them? Do any of these issues mesh well into my Candidate Message Grid on the next page? Pick three.
   1. _____
   2. _____
   3. _____

Exercise 2: The Candidate's Message Grid

While crafting your story, it can be helpful to compare and contrast yourself with your opponents. This chart is called the Candidate Grid. This grid can help you frame any campaign, plan your message, and map out your opponent's possible responses.

Sample Candidate's Message Grid

	John McCain	Barack Obama
John McCain	**McCain on McCain** 1. War hero 2. Strong, stable 3. Experienced 4. Maverick, willing to vote against party and self-interests 5. Puts his country and the common good first.	**McCain on Obama** 1. No military experience 2. Weak, unstable 3. Inexperienced 4. Chicago party machine 5. Votes according to popular opinion polls and to please radical elements
Barack Obama	**Obama on McCain** 1. Warmonger who has been damaged by war experiences 2. Hot-tempered 3. Stuck in the past 4. Erratic, unpredictable 5. A good man at heart who is "out of touch" with reality	**Obama on Obama** 1. Community Leader 2. Strong, Innovative 3. Brings Change 4. Fought his party his entire career 5. A new kind of leader for America's new century

My Message Grid

	Me	Opponent
	Me on Me	**Me on Opponent**
Me	1. _____ 2. _____ 3. _____ 4. _____ 5. _____	1. _____ 2. _____ 3. _____ 4. _____ 5. _____
	Opponent on Me	**Opponent on Opponent**
Opponent	1. _____ 2. _____ 3. _____ 4. _____ 5. _____	1. _____ 2. _____ 3. _____ 4. _____ 5. _____

Exercise 3: Partisan Politics

The Partisan Politics Spectrum is another tool to help you construct your message and explain it to others.

Republican vs. Independent

The Republican vs. Independent, Libertarian, or Constitutionalist race is very common in exurbia and rural communities. These races tend to occur in regions of the country that are more conservative than average. The key to winning these types of races in conservative havens is to appear even more fiscally responsible. Emphasize that you want an even smaller and less intrusive government that respects gun and property rights.

When thinking about and explaining your strategy and message, draw a line like this:

Republican vs. Independent Spectrum (Example)

Democrat	Republican	Me

Big Government   Small Government
High Taxes   Very Low Taxes
Regulations   Property Rights

My Spectrum – Filled in with local issues.

Democrat	Republican	Me

_____

_____

_____

_____

Democrat vs. Independent

Democrat vs. Independent races are very common in big city urban environments, especially on the East and West coasts, or in rural areas that still vote for old-fashioned Democrats. If you are fighting an old fashion Democrat in a rural area, use the same strategy as Republican vs. Independent. In big city urban areas, the race is most likely to be more liberal than average. The key to winning liberal strongholds is to emphasize your support for civil liberties, no government regulation of marriage, and drug re-legalization. Portray your Democratic opponent as less committed to these ideas as you.

Democrat vs. Independent Spectrum (Example)

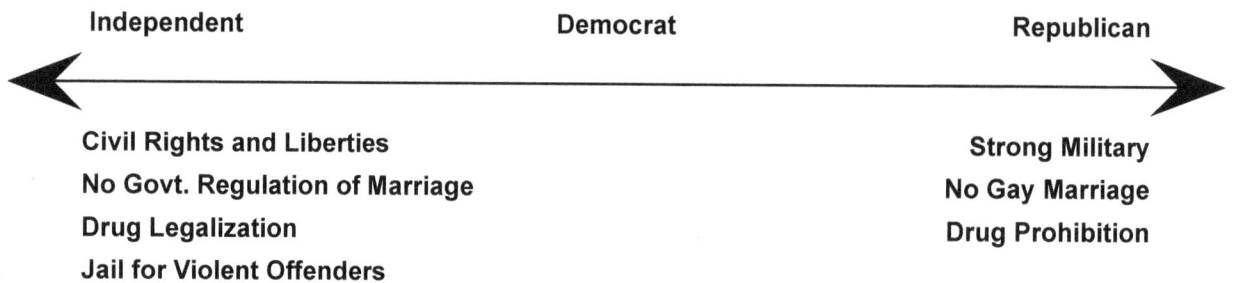

Independent	Democrat	Republican

←————————————————————————————→

Civil Rights and Liberties   **Strong Military**
No Govt. Regulation of Marriage   **No Gay Marriage**
Drug Legalization   **Drug Prohibition**
Jail for Violent Offenders

My Spectrum – Filled in with local issues.

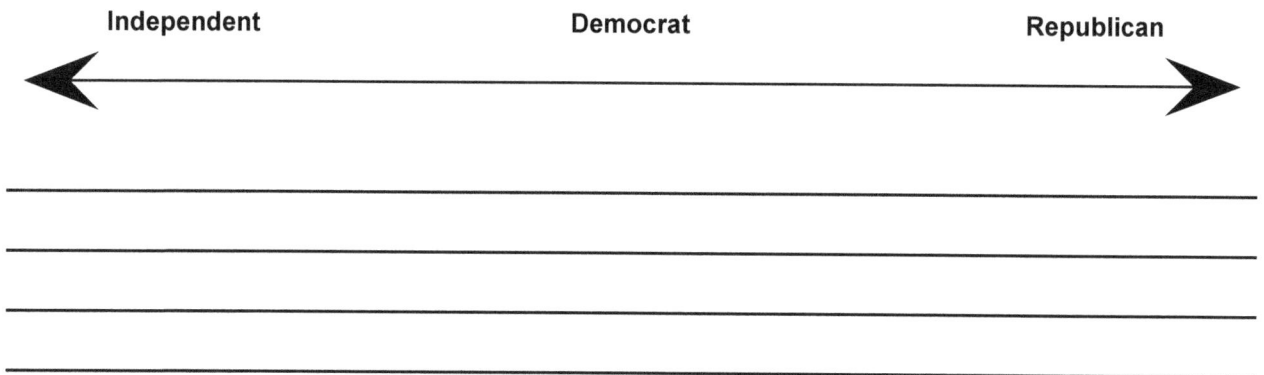

Independent	Democrat	Republican

←————————————————————————————→

_____

_____

_____

_____

Republican vs. Democrat vs. Independent

The issues listed previously under two-party races are called "wedge issues." An ideal wedge issue divides your opponent's base of support while solidifying your own base. In three-way races it is exceedingly difficult to hit both Democrats and Republicans with successful wedges. In this situation you need a "double wedge" issue. Emphasize the negative issues both Democrats and Republicans have in common. Focus on the "sameness" of the two parties and attack their unfair monopoly on political power.

Republican vs. Democrat vs. Independent Spectrum (Example)

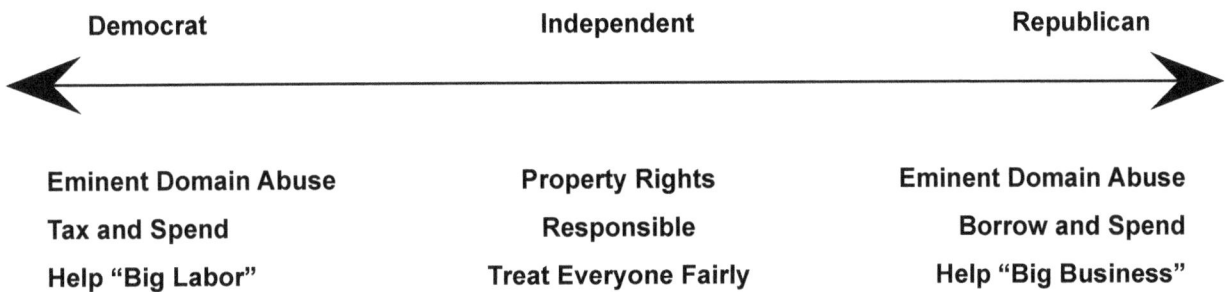

Democrat	Independent	Republican
Eminent Domain Abuse	Property Rights	Eminent Domain Abuse
Tax and Spend	Responsible	Borrow and Spend
Help "Big Labor"	Treat Everyone Fairly	Help "Big Business"

My Spectrum - Filled in with local issues.

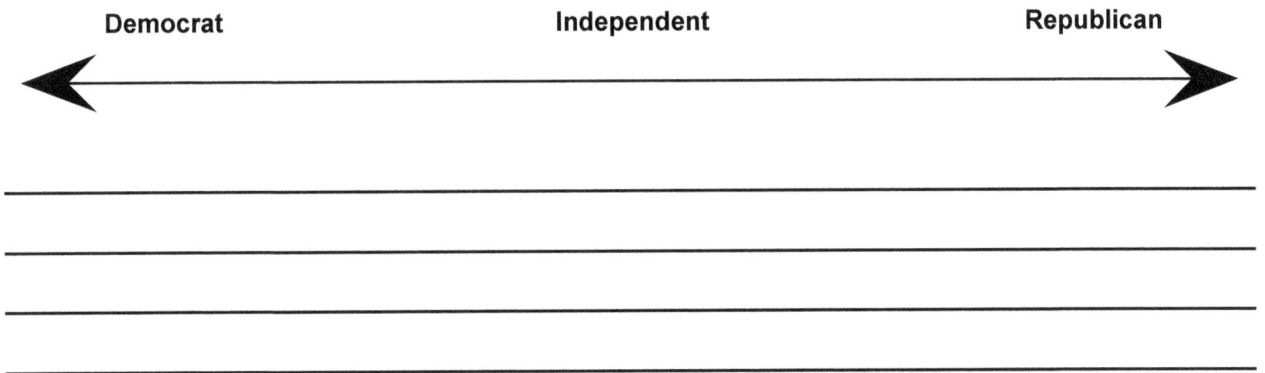

Democrat	Independent	Republican

_____

_____

_____

_____

NOTES:

18 Steps to Win a Local Election

Step 13:

Advertise My Answer

Now that you have fleshed out your message, you are ready to produce advertising for the campaign. Paid advertising is any piece of promotional material for a campaign including print, audio, video, and website information produced to influence public opinion. Paid advertising differs from earned media in that it is produced, distributed, and paid for directly by the campaign. You earn the earned media by doing something that is deemed newsworthy. This is also called free media.

Paid Advertising Checklist

☐ I have bought what I absolutely need first: business cards, website, name tags.

☐ I designed and agreed on a color scheme and logo before making any purchases.

☐ I will maintain the same look, color scheme, and logo on all promotional items.

☐ I shop around for the best prices and negotiate better deals.

☐ I always have something professional to hand out wherever I go.

☐ Yard signs are usually a high priority in local races. I have calculated how many I need and where they will go for the most impact.

☐ I have appointed a volunteer sign coordinator who will keep track of who has yard signs and where they are being posted. I will have a plan for distribution of signs at polling places on Election Day and a retrieval plan. Usually the posts can be re-used. There may be local ordinances and fines for failure to remove signs after Election Day.

☐ I will beware of the sign wars. In recent years, the number of citizens and campaigns stealing each other's signs has reached a fever pitch. I will not retaliate in kind. The very best way to deal with this problem is to videotape the perpetrator and give the tape to my local news stations and papers.

☐ All my materials are easy to read (signs from far away while driving).

☐ I will saturate my market with one kind of advertising before moving on. For example: sending three direct mail pieces to my target audience vs. sending one direct piece to everyone.

☐ All of my paid advertising materials are working together to attract attention and present one unifying campaign theme supported by three big issues. The promotional give-aways, fliers, postcards, brochures, yard signs, radio commercials, TV commercials, online videos, and website are all working together to 1) attract attention and 2) present one clear message.

☐ Promotional give-aways (magnets, pencils, notepads, nail files, etc.) are memorable, tasteful, and useful. People will want to keep and use them.

☐ I have made sure that every item that needs a legal disclaimer will have one.

☐ I have opened a web store so my supporters have access to campaign materials and can help me pay for them, but I still give away freebies to everyone else.

☐ I have a system in place to make sure that advertising is reaching the intended audience (i.e. check with friends to see if they received postcards or phone calls, etc.).

☐ I have distinct paid advertising directed towards my three consumer groups: contributors, volunteers, and voters.

☐ I have checked what previous candidates for this office have spent on previous campaigns to see what works in my area.

☐ I am checking my opponents' advertising to find out what their message is, who they are sending it to, and how much they are spending.

☐ I am adjusting my methods or my message in response to my opponents' if it is necessary and only after careful consideration with my advisors.

☐ Every item has at least one, and preferably multiple, contact methods to connect with the campaign.

☐ Every item tells a visual story in support of the written theme.

Website Design Checklist

Every candidate must have a website. It has become expected and unavoidable. Since it is considered so easy and cheap, not having a website raises serious concerns about whether a campaign is "for real." The first thing nearly every consumer tells a candidate is: "Everything you say sounds great. Is there a website where I can get more information?" Most consumers now prefer to get at least some of their information from the web. Here is a list of helpful website design tips.

- ☐ My site addresses voters' concerns, it's not just about how great I am.

- ☐ I designed my site to meet the needs of my visitors, not just my organization.

- ☐ Anyone can understand what the site is about in four seconds and find the focal point of the page.

- ☐ The website's domain name is short, relevant, easy to remember, and easy to read from far away or in moving vehicle.

- ☐ My content is current and updated frequently, and I put dates on material that's not updated regularly.

- ☐ I have a distinct media page where reporters can quickly find my campaign bio, a high resolution picture, and my cell phone (or the communications director's cell phone) for quick interviews.

- ☐ All of my press releases and favorable news articles are available and easy to find on the media page.

- ☐ My site makes the campaign staff look like credible professionals.

- ☐ My home page — or any page — doesn't take more than four seconds to load.

- ☐ I am collecting all the data from my volunteers and contributors that I need for my own internal purposes and the legal requirements.

- ☐ I have made it easy and secure to contribute money online.

- ☐ I always conduct user testing and analyze my log files. (Log files tell you how long someone visits each page, which pages they view, and which page they exit from.)

- [ ] My website isn't just a brochure. It is interactive, and people have a reason to return because they can plan their own campaign events, check the candidate's calendar, and build a community of friends with common ideological backgrounds.

- [ ] I have regular weekly reports at my campaign meeting to discuss how many people have seen my website, which pages are the most popular, and how much money I have raised online.

- [ ] My website has a regularly updated blog where someone from the campaign writes about what happened that day (or week).

- [ ] I am constantly thinking of ways to improve, but I am not completely redesigning the website each week.

- [ ] My website directs visitors to email their local media outlets to express their positive support for my campaign and makes it easy for them to do so.

- [ ] Quickly scanning the page tells my visitors about its purpose.

- [ ] I have eliminated unnecessary or distracting design items.

- [ ] I have checked to see if my site looks the same and performs well in all the major browsers.

- [ ] My pages do not have too much or too little white space.

- [ ] My site does not mix up text sizes and colors on the page.

- [ ] I put design elements where visitors expect them.

- [ ] Logo and contact information is on the top of every page and clicking it leads to the home or contact page.

- [ ] Visited links change color.

- [ ] I identify PDF files with an icon.

- [ ] My logo looks like it was professionally made and is proportional to the screen.

- [ ] My site works when visited with the JavaScript turned off.

- [ ] My site has a campaign calendar that lets visitors know where I will be and can send out email reminders to events they have RSVP'ed to.

- [ ] The important content fits in the first screen.

- [ ] My site uses a white or off-white color for background.

- [ ] My site has a search engine and its box is long enough to see what you have typed.

- [ ] Underlined text is always a link.

☐ I regularly check to see if my site's links are broken.

☐ My site's content is in plain English and only necessary jargon or acronyms are present with links to their definitions.

☐ I use a consistent tone throughout. I don't switch back and forth from colloquial to scientific, etc.

☐ I have our legal disclaimer across the bottom of every page.

☐ My site invites visitor feedback.

☐ I use email to keep my supporters excited and informed, solicit financial contributions, and encourage and direct volunteer efforts. I will email my supporters regularly. As often as once per week is not unexpected.

NOTES:

Step 14:
Become the News

"Don't pick a fight with anyone who buys ink by the barrel and paper by the ton."
- Mark Twain

Cultivating media contacts is simpler than it may appear. Before you ever decide to run for office or volunteer to be an organization's media contact, offer to make an appointment to meet with your political reporters. (Buy them lunch if you can.)

Become the News Checklist

☐ To become the news, I must do, tell, or expose newsworthy stories. Most candidates who fail to get headlines are often not doing anything interesting enough to merit them.

☐ If I am running a micro-campaign for the township water board or planning commission, I may only get two mentions in the paper: once when I declare and once when I win. But I can turn this around by doing my own research, attending the board meetings, and writing news releases that tell interesting stories.

☐ The news media is in the sales business. I can overcome bias by becoming more interesting and exciting. Entertaining candidates sell newspapers—publicity events can be a big help!

☐ As a responsible and professional candidate, I will hold my own credibility and that of my party or fellow Independents in my hands. I will always have direct evidence to support my story readily available (especially at a press conference).

☐ My relationship with the newspaper is very important in shaping the coverage I receive from other news organizations.

☐ Television news and the news wire services such as Reuters and Associated Press will immediately pick up any story published in my major daily newspaper so I do not need to pay for any news wire services.

☐ Reporters work on very strict schedules and deadlines. My job as a candidate or campaign manager is to make a reporter's job to cover the candidate as easy as possible. This means writing and distributing press releases which can be used nearly word for word.

☐ I will write the article in the same style as the newspaper and include some contrary viewpoints. My entire release may be cut and pasted into tomorrow's paper.

☐ The paper will assign one or possibly two political reporters to cover the race. It is important for me to meet these reporters early and establish trust. I can normally predict who a reporter will be by reading similar political stories from the neighborhood and checking the bylines.

☐ I will find out how the reporter prefers to receive my press releases. Most prefer faxes or emails. I will always call the reporter to be sure a news release has been received, especially faxes. I will also ask if he or she is able to come to any scheduled press conferences. I will offer to change my schedule if there is a conflict, as it is likely I will also lose television stations if another event is happening.

☐ The key to television news is usually the assignment desk. The assignment desk is responsible for sending reporters and cameras into the field. My challenge is to convince the assignment editor that my news is among the most important of the day and will look good on television.

☐ It is expensive to send camera crews to a location, and stations typically have only one to three crews available on any given day. If I waste their time, I may never get a second opportunity.

☐ The farther the scheduled event is from the station, the less likely a crew will come to the event. Most crews will travel a half hour with no problem.

☐ My best chance to get television time is to schedule my event for a slow news day. Wednesdays and Thursdays are typically the slowest, but I will check around with other reporters and call the assignment desk to see if another time may be better.

☐ I will find out if anything important is going on at the national, state, or local level before I schedule a press conference. I don't want to be bumped out of the line-up.

☐ I visit locally operated non-dailies in person to introduce myself. I may also wish to indicate my interest in buying advertising and how much I am planning to spend. This will do wonders for my local coverage. (There is no other reason for a candidate to pay for newspaper ads.)

☐ Most radio stations do not have stand-alone news operations. If a radio station is part of a larger broadcast company, the television news people may broadcast on their channel. Otherwise, most radio stations simply read the news from the AP wire service or even from the newspaper.

☐ If I live near a large city, I will probably have a few reporters at a local public radio station. There may also be talk radio broadcast in the area. It is usually a great idea to appear on local talk radio stations, but I will be sure the host is at least somewhat favorable to my cause. Otherwise, I will find myself insulted and interrupted with no way to defend myself. Most talk radio thrives on controversy—be careful.

☐ I have assembled a professional campaign media kit that includes: a candidate bio, a statement of my campaign theme and three most important issues, a physical and electronic copy of my professional headshot, a physical and electronic copy of several good action shots, my campaign promotional materials, and contact information for me and my communications director. I will definitely include my cell phone number. Media calls can come at any time and must be answered immediately.

Exercise 1: Cultivate Media Contacts

Local Newspapers

1. Newspaper:

_____

Name   Physical Address

_____

Mailing Address

Political Editor: _____

Name   Email   Phone   Fax

Preferred Method of Contact: ☐ Email   ☐ Fax

Notes: _____

_____

_____

_____

Political Reporter: _____

Name   Email   Phone   Fax

Preferred Method of Contact: ☐ Email   ☐ Fax

Notes: _____

_____

_____

_____

2. Newspaper: _____

          Name   Physical Address

_____

          Mailing Address

Political Editor: _____

          Name   Email   Phone   Fax

Preferred Method of Contact: ☐ Email   ☐ Fax

        Notes: _____

_____

_____

Political Reporter: _____

          Name   Email   Phone   Fax

Preferred Method of Contact: ☐ Email   ☐ Fax

        Notes: _____

_____

_____

3. Newspaper: _____

          Name   Physical Address

_____

          Mailing Address

Political Editor: _____

          Name   Email   Phone   Fax

Preferred Method of Contact: ☐ Email   ☐ Fax

        Notes: _____

_____

_____

Political Reporter: _____

          Name   Email   Phone   Fax

Preferred Method of Contact: ☐ Email   ☐ Fax

        Notes: _____

_____

_____

Local Broadcast

1. Television: _____
Name   Physical Studio Address

_____
Mailing Address

Political Editor: _____
Name   Email   Phone   Fax

Preferred Method of Contact: ☐ Email   ☐ Fax

Notes: _____

_____

_____

Political Reporter: _____
Name   Email   Phone   Fax

Preferred Method of Contact: ☐ Email   ☐ Fax

Notes: _____

_____

_____

2. Television: _____
Name   Physical Studio Address

_____
Mailing Address

Political Editor: _____
Name   Email   Phone   Fax

Preferred Method of Contact: ☐ Email   ☐ Fax

Notes: _____

_____

_____

Political Reporter: _____
Name   Email   Phone   Fax

Preferred Method of Contact: ☐ Email   ☐ Fax

Notes: _____

_____

_____

3. Television:

_____
Name   Physical Studio Address

_____
Mailing Address

Political Editor: _____
Name   Email   Phone   Fax

Preferred Method of Contact: ☐ Email   ☐ Fax

Notes: _____

_____

_____

Political Reporter: _____
Name   Email   Phone   Fax

Preferred Method of Contact: ☐ Email   ☐ Fax

Notes: _____

_____

_____

4. Television:

_____
Name   Physical Studio Address

_____
Mailing Address

Political Editor: _____
Name   Email   Phone   Fax

Preferred Method of Contact: ☐ Email   ☐ Fax

Notes: _____

_____

_____

Political Reporter: _____
Name   Email   Phone   Fax

Preferred Method of Contact: ☐ Email   ☐ Fax

Notes: _____

_____

_____

1. Local NPR Station: _____

Name   Physical Studio Address

_____

Mailing Address

Radio Producer: _____

Name   Email   Phone   Fax

Preferred Method of Contact: ☐ Email   ☐ Fax

Notes: _____

_____

_____

Radio Reporter: _____

Name   Email   Phone   Fax

Preferred Method of Contact: ☐ Email   ☐ Fax

Notes: _____

_____

_____

2. Local NPR Station: _____

Name   Physical Studio Address

_____

Mailing Address

Radio Producer: _____

Name   Email   Phone   Fax

Preferred Method of Contact: ☐ Email   ☐ Fax

Notes: _____

_____

_____

Radio Reporter: _____

Name   Email   Phone   Fax

Preferred Method of Contact: ☐ Email   ☐ Fax

Notes: _____

_____

_____

1. Local Talk Radio:

Name	Physical Studio Address

Mailing Address

Radio Producer:

Name	Email	Phone	Fax

Preferred Method of Contact: ☐ Email   ☐ Fax

Notes: _____

_____

Radio Reporter:

Name	Email	Phone	Fax

Preferred Method of Contact: ☐ Email   ☐ Fax

Notes: _____

_____

2. Local Talk Radio:

Name	Physical Studio Address

Mailing Address

Radio Producer:

Name	Email	Phone	Fax

Preferred Method of Contact: ☐ Email   ☐ Fax

Notes: _____

_____

Radio Reporter:

Name	Email	Phone	Fax

Preferred Method of Contact: ☐ Email   ☐ Fax

Notes: _____

_____

Exercise 2: Write a News Release and Set up a News Conference

It may sound intimidating or self-important to write a news release or call a press conference, but it's really not a big deal.

News Release and Conference Checklist

- [ ] I read and watch the news regularly and take note of the technical details.

- [ ] A news release should be direct and similar in style to articles in the local newspaper. I will keep it to one page.

- [ ] News releases are about action. Letters to the editor or op-eds are opinions.

- [ ] I only write news releases about an action someone is doing. I do not write a news release about what someone thinks or says. That is only an opinion.

- [ ] I always follow the proper news release format (as shown after this list).

- [ ] A story needs a conflict; I tell both sides of the story in a way that is favorable to the candidate.

- [ ] I include quotations for and against the main story. I pick a weak argument for my against quote.

- [ ] I am always in favor of something. I change negative statements into positives. For example, "Candidate to Cut Taxes," not "Candidate Against Taxes."

- [ ] Whether my race is large or small, I organize a news conference for my announcement. This may be my only news conference in a micro-campaign, and it may only attract print reporters.

- [ ] Candidates for mayor or city council typically generate much more publicity even in small towns. One press release per week and one conference per month are not unusual.

- [ ] Each news release contains only one main idea (one news story). If I have several good newsworthy ideas, I spread them out over the course of the campaign in multiple releases.

- [ ] A news conference is called when a story is so big that a simple release is not enough.

- [ ] It is the campaign's responsibility to generate big stories and keep the campaign interesting for media, voters, volunteers, and financial contributors.

☐ Press conferences should be fun and exciting. I invite and encourage all volunteers to be present and act as cheerleaders. My volunteers should wear their campaign t-shirts, if possible.

☐ I always have a staff member (not the candidate) confirm whether someone received the release and ask if they are planning to attend the conference or have any further questions.

☐ Professionalism with the news media is vital. If I waste someone's time, that may be the last opportunity I have. I don't call reporters in the late afternoon. That is their deadline, and they are busy. I always start a conversation by asking a reporter if they have time to talk.

☐ Pictures speak louder than words on television. First, I am sure to choose a location easily accessible to the media. I pay very close attention to what appears behind you in the camera shot. Is it the image I want for myself and this story?

☐ I write down what I have to say in advance, and memorize it until I am comfortable speaking without notes. I have an outline of my main points in an oversized font at my podium. I am sure to start with a few short punchy sentences that encapsulate everything I want my audience to understand. I have developed a sentence rhythm: short, short, long, short, short, long.

☐ The campaign manager or communications director should stand behind the cameras and reporters to offer direction to the candidate if needed. For example, a manager may hastily scribble SPEAK INTO THE MIC in large block letters on a sheet of paper or MENTION THE HOSPITAL.

☐ I work out hand signals in advance so that the manager can give immediate feedback while I am speaking.

☐ I anticipate questions and practice answering them with my staff. (Hold a mock conference.)

Campaign Logo Goes Here
Campaign Address, Website
Date

FOR IMMEDIATE RELEASE

NEWS RELEASE (or NEWS CONFERENCE)

Contact: Communication Director's Name
(Office) (123) 456-7890
(Cell) (123) 456-7890
Email: communications@campaign.org

TIME: (Date and Time of New Conference)
LOCATION: (Location of News Conference)

MAIN TITLE OF NEWS RELEASE IN CAPS
Subheading in Upper and Lower Case

This sentence grabs attention with a clear statement of bold action from candidate. This sentence adds some details. Adds some details.

"A visionary candidate quote," said the candidate.

More details about the story. More details about the story. More details about the story. More details about the story.

"Someone with a contrary view and a weak argument is quoted here."

More details about the story. More details about the story.

"Candidate slams the door on the weak argument. Candidate does not personally attack speaker of argument."

"Campaign Manager says campaign is the best thing since sliced bread."

# # #

For more information please visit our website or call John Smith, Communications Director, at (123) 456-7890. John Smith's email address goes here.

NOTES:

Step 15:

Attend Public Events

You can also generate positive publicity by attending public events or staging your own. It is important to notify the media with a press release when you are making a public appearance. Try to get endorsements! Some organizations have rules against political speakers, but you can still attend as an audience member and speak with members privately. Your scheduler should work the phones and make these happen!

Public Events or Meetings

- Rotary Club, Lions Club, Kiwanis Club
- School and professional sporting events, parades
- Meetings and conferences of professional associations
- Union meetings, especially the Fraternal Order of Police
- Chamber of Commerce meetings, morning coffees, after hours drinks
- League of Women Voters meetings, forums, and debates
- High School and College social studies classes
- The public meetings of the person I wish to replace (City Council, etc.)

Your Own Publicity Events

- Make an official campaign announcement
- Turn in petition signatures
- Put together a concert, a family picnic, a pig roast, a ballot initiative, etc.
- Lead a march or a rally
- Cast your own ballot

Candidate Forums and Debates Checklist

☐ My scheduler and volunteers need to be on the lookout. I will not always get invited to forums and debates.

☐ Before attending any forum or debate, I practice answering questions with my staff. Together, we should be able to anticipate most of the questions. I always begin my answer by restating the question and explaining the answer in terms that would make sense to any fourth grader.

☐ I craft the best possible answers and practice those answers until they become second nature. I memorize specific facts and figures to back up my opinions. I have a thirty second, two minute, and five minute answer.

☐ I am here to tell my story. I make sure that is the priority. When I make my opening statements, and whenever I answer a question, I am sure to tie in my unique story and background. I am lively, entertaining, and humorous.

☐ These events typically take place on a September or October evening at the local community center, VFW hall, or public library.

☐ These events are essentially a job interview in which I and my opponent will stand side by side to appeal for votes, present our strengths, and explain our opinions on local issues.

☐ I look my best and wear my best suit.

☐ I take someone with me to help distribute materials and watch my performance. I may want to record this event for my website, but I must find out if this is permitted first.

☐ I am gracious and magnanimous to my hosts and opponent. Nasty or rude comments will not win votes, even if my opponent deserves them.

☐ I bring volunteer sign-up sheets, pledge cards, business cards, and printed material (flier, post card, slim jim, etc.)

☐ After the event is over, I analyze my performance with my staff who attended the event. Did I stay on message? Did I answer the questions? Did my message resonate with the audience? Was my delivery on target? I will improve and learn from each event.

NOTES:

NOTES:

18 Steps to Win a Local Election

Step 16:

Go Door-to-Door

The Door-to-Door Checklist

☐ As a local candidate, I plan on campaigning door-to-door at least three days per week. Weekday evenings are usually best.

☐ Volunteers should accompany the candidate as much as possible. I pair volunteers of the opposite sex to walk together. Women will be hesitant to open their doors to solitary men. Volunteers should be clearly identified.

☐ The first step in any door-to-door campaign is identifying and sorting communities in three sections: favorable precincts, swing precincts, and unfavorable precincts.

☐ Where I go depends on my campaign strategy. If I am a new, relatively unknown candidate, I will need to visit precincts I predict to be favorable to introduce myself. This will strengthen my base and give me an idea of how favorable the precinct really is.

☐ I will also need to visit the swing precincts. This is my opportunity to convince undecided or otherwise persuadable voters. Swing voters and Independents vote for candidates, not parties, so I will have an excellent chance to win their votes.

☐ If I am running in a two-way campaign, I consider that most voters of the other party will vote for me if I can get them to the polling place.

☐ After deciding which neighborhoods to walk, I assemble a walking list before going out. (Refer to the next exercise: Assemble My Walking List)

☐ Feedback received from my door-to-door campaign is used to refine my message, especially if a continuing pattern emerges.

☐ When I am finished walking for the day, I gather my data and that of the volunteers. I give my cards to my database person or the designated organizer right away.

Exercise 1: Assemble a Walking List

In Step 6, you examined your own community. You divided your precincts into three groups: favorable, swing, and unfavorable.

Your database person will sort the voter database you obtain from the local Elections Office into these favorable, swing, and unfavorable precincts.

Once you have separated the favorable precincts you will sort those voters according to their voting history. The amount of time you have to go door-to-door, the size of your electorate, and the number of volunteers you have will determine whether you can visit every voter or just those who have voted in the last four to six years. Plan and decide this with your staff.

After you have separated out who you will visit, you need to sort them into walking order. Some computer programs can do this for you. But you can usually do a pretty good job manually by separating the even and odd numbered houses into two piles.

The walking list should be printed on labels and stuck to index cards. If multiple voters live in the same house, stick their stickers on just one card. These index cards will have some questions you would like to ask each voter. An easy way to make your own question cards is with a photocopier and cardstock.

Questions should have something to do with your message and help identify issues important to the community. Questions should be yes or no, or positive or negative.

The answers on your card will be a scale from one to five. A one indicates highly negative, a two: somewhat negative, a three: neutral or doesn't know, a four: somewhat positive, and a five: highly positive.

Circle the name of the voter you spoke to or write his or her name if not listed. Correct the cards if the voter listed has died or moved. Be sure to get the new names. This data is extremely important and valuable to your campaign as well as to your local and state parties. Take the time to get it right.

You now have data which enables you to target voters at the individual level. You can customize your mailings. It is especially important to stop wasting time and money on decided voters. People who love and like you need to be saved for GOTV. Continue mailing and phoning the positives. You don't want them to forget you. People who hate and dislike you should be removed from future mailings and phone calls. In aggregate, these numbers can give you the pulse of the community. It is important to check voters' responses to your message. If they seem apathetic or hostile to it, then you need to find out why and fix it.

Ask your favorables if you can email them a reminder to vote and ask for their email address. Offer a ride to anyone who needs it on Election Day.

Remind your favorables when and where to vote while you are visiting them.

Sample Walking List Index Card

Here is an example of a walking list card. It indicates that a man and a woman live at the address (confirm that), their address, their telephone number, their party registration, their precinct number, and the place where they vote.

John Smith (123) 456-7890	Mary Smith (123) 456-7890
123 Main St. Smithville 21345	123 Main St. Smithville 21345
Republican	Democrat
Precinct 22 – Our Savior Church	Precinct 22 – Our Savior Church

1. How do you feel about our current city councilman?   1 2 3 4 5

2. Did you approve of the tax increase?   1 2 3 4 5

3. Did you think it was a good idea to borrow $100 million to build a new City Hall?   1 2 3 4 5

4. Would you like to better financial accountability?   1 2 3 4 5

5. Can I count on your vote on November 4th?   1 2 3 4 5

6. Is it ok if I send you an email reminder to vote?   _____

NOTES:

18 Steps to Win a Local Election

Step 17:

Get Out the Vote (GOTV)

Phone Operation

Four days before Election Day, your volunteers need to begin calling those who need a ride to confirm a time and place for pick-up. Here is a sample script. Feel free to alter the script for your campaign.

Supporters Who Need a Ride Script

Volunteer: "Hello. This is _____ calling on behalf of Fred Jones for Mayor. According to our records, you indicated you may need a ride on Election Day. We're really counting on your support to put our campaign over the top. Do you need any assistance getting to the polls this Tuesday?"

(If yes): "We have volunteers who have offered to drive people to the polls on Election Day. I would be happy to schedule a driver to pick you up. Can you please tell me when would be a good time? And where should our driver meet you? Ok. We will be sending a driver at _____(time) on Election Day to meet you at _____(address). Do you have a pen handy? Please call _____ if you have any questions or need to cancel or change your pick-up. Thank you for your time. Have a good day."

(If no): "We have plenty of volunteers who would be happy to help you. Are you sure you can get to the polls ok? Alright, can I give you our phone number in case you change your mind? It's _____. Have a nice day."

On the day or the weekend before the election, your volunteers should begin calling all likely voters who scored favorable to your campaign. Remind them to vote on Election Day. If your phone volunteers run through their list, they can call a second time.

Volunteer: "Hello. This is _____ calling on behalf of Fred Jones for Mayor. We are counting on your vote to help put us over the top. We feel we have a really good chance to make a strong showing in this election, but we really need you to go vote this Tuesday for Fred Jones. Can we count on your vote?"

(If yes): "Do you need a ride to your polling place? (If yes see above). Thank you for your support. Have a great day."

- The phone volunteers are the best resource for reaching every voter multiple times.
- There is a certain psychology to telephone volunteers. They work best in groups in phone banks.
- A phone bank can be as simple as several folding tables surrounded by chairs and a multitude of phone lines. There are now many kinds of cable, internet, and virtual phone companies; check around.
- Invite volunteers with free weekend and night minutes on their cell phones to come in to the phone bank.
- Phone volunteers can be used to target different types of voters with your different messages, fundraise, organize rides for GOTV, and remind your favorables to vote on Election Day.
- Create some fun incentives for your phone volunteers. Maybe a local business can contribute prizes to the volunteers who do the most work.
- Thank your volunteers regularly by ordering pizza, providing beverages, throwing a party, etc.

The Election Day Checklist

On Election Day, you have finally reached the last inning, but don't take your eye off the ball. There are several simple but complicated operations that need to go smoothly. Every person in the campaign should plan to spend most, if not all, of the day at a precinct polling place handing out palm cards or driving people to the polls. The Election Night party is the best time to thank everyone and have a good time.

The Candidate

☐ I will remain calm and cool during this potentially stressful day. The campaign staff should help put me at ease.

☐ I should vote at the opening time in my polling location and be sure the media have been invited to see me.

☐ I plan to be at the highest priority polling location all day shaking hands and passing out palm cards.

- ☐ I will make sure cell phone is fully charged the night before.

- ☐ I will have a volunteer to assist me throughout the day and carry a cellular phone. Under no circumstances should I attempt to shake hands while speaking on the phone.

- ☐ I should be prepared to leave the polling place to do television interviews if necessary. All other interviews should be conducted by phone.

- ☐ After the polls close, I should take a quick shower before the Election Night party.

- ☐ At the election party, I will thank my family, friends, and supporters who have believed in me.

The Campaign Manager

- ☐ I will meet with everyone before Election Day to plan out each person's assigned tasks.

- ☐ I will determine which polling places will have the most favorable and swing voters on Election Day. These will be my highest priority polling places where I must have volunteers present.

- ☐ I will create maps indicating all of the polling places voting in this race and distribute these maps to the volunteers. I will assign each volunteer a place.

- ☐ I should plan to work at the second highest priority polling location or assist in GOTV as much as possible.

- ☐ I should be sure that the Election Day operation is running smoothly and be in regular contact with the staff.

- ☐ I will keep the candidate calm and on schedule. I will make sure the candidate has the best assistant.

- ☐ I will make sure that everyone has a charged cell phone and a list of the contacts they need.

- ☐ I will make sure that people carry their cameras and video cameras in their cars. There will be memorable moments and possible legal actions.

- ☐ I will be prepared to call the Secretary of State or the county elections officials in case of problems at the polling places. I will be calm and firm. I will document irregularities with cameras and eyewitness accounts.

- ☐ This is the day for maximum delegation of authority and volunteer effort. I will hold a meeting the night before the election and make sure everyone knows their designated task. The manager can't possibly do everything or be everywhere on Election Day.

The Volunteer Coordinator

☐ Before the election, I need to meet with the volunteers to explain the plan for Election Day. I will assign each volunteer (except the phone volunteers) a precinct place according to priority.

☐ I will make sure the phone bank is working smoothly. I will be sure that the phone volunteers have all the correct phone numbers and scripts they need.

☐ I need to check volunteer attendance at the precinct polling places in person. I should also be sure the precinct volunteers have adequate signs, materials, water, and snacks.

☐ At lunch time, I should deliver lunch so that the volunteers can stay on location all day. Sometimes, campaigns use high school or college students to volunteer at polling locations. I will offer these students food if I see them without it; they may switch to supporting my campaign. Many times, a business owner friendly to the campaign will provide box lunches for free or at a reduced rate for volunteers on Election Day.

☐ I will make sure my cell phone is powered up today. Everyone should be calling me if they have any difficulty. If my volunteers have a problem with poll workers, I need to check out the problem personally. I will see if a serious law is being broken or if there is just a simple difference of opinion. If the problem seriously interferes with the election and I cannot resolve the issue with the on-site leader of the poll workers, it is time to phone the Elections Office to notify them directly. In many cases, the poll workers are volunteers and may misunderstand the law.

☐ I will not waste time arguing over how far I am standing from the polling place. Every precinct leader seems to have a different concept of distance. As long as all the campaigns are treated equally, there isn't much I can do.

☐ I will document any election irregularity. I will take photos and get names.

☐ As night approaches, I will prepare for the election night party. I will take a quick shower if needed and prepare the party location. I will get some volunteers to help.

Phone Volunteers

☐ Phone volunteers should spend the day calling registered voters who have previously indicated at least some support for the campaign.

☐ They need to remind favorables that today is Election Day and where they should go to vote. They should also ask if the voter needs assistance in getting to the polls.

☐ Volunteers need maps of where people vote and the ability to call the drivers.

Volunteer Drivers

- ☐ Volunteer drivers are going to be the campaign's taxi/shuttle bus service.

- ☐ These volunteers need to be given specific instructions on when and where to pick up voters and have maps of all the polling locations.

- ☐ These drivers need to have radios or cell phones so they can report back to their coordinator and receive last minute information.

- ☐ Drivers should stay in the same neighboring precincts if possible.

- ☐ Drivers should have magnetic signs or some other type of identification on their cars and on their person (t-shirt or name tag).

- ☐ It is best to use cars or vans that are easy to enter and exit. They should be clean and professional. Keep adequate supplies of campaign materials in the vehicle for people to read and allow them to show their support with stickers.

Precinct Volunteers

- ☐ The campaign manager needs to determine which precincts have the highest priority. Working together with the volunteer coordinator, the manager should plan to have at least two volunteers at each polling place beginning with the highest priority locations.

- ☐ High priority precincts are determined by the number of expected voters and the expected level of support. Mixed and undecided precincts with large numbers of voters are the highest priority. Your favorable precincts are the next highest, and your opponent's or small precincts are the lowest priority.

- ☐ Volunteers should stand near the polling place, distribute literature, shake hands, and encourage people to vote for the candidate.

- ☐ Volunteers should all wear a campaign t-shirt, sticker, or button.

- ☐ All volunteers must know the laws concerning where to stand and what can be done on Election Day at the polling places.

- ☐ Precinct volunteers should make sure that every polling place has campaign signs posted at the lawful distance.

- ☐ Volunteers need to remember that the official poll workers determine how the rules will be enforced. Volunteers should never argue with a poll worker or election official. If a problem arises, volunteers should be instructed to call the volunteer coordinator or the campaign manager and have a list of phone numbers to call in an emergency.

- ☐ Any irregularity should be documented. Take photos and get names.

- ☐ Volunteers should agree to work a specific schedule, preferably all day. Most people come to vote during rush hour: from opening time to 10AM and from 3PM to closing time.

The Finance Director

☐ I will be sure to call all major contributors, thank them for their support, and confirm that they will vote.

☐ I will get together with the treasurer and find out how many outstanding debts are remaining. Today is the last best chance to raise extra money for the campaign.

☐ At the Election Night party, I will announce any outstanding debts and pass the hat if necessary.

The Communications Director

☐ I will send press releases the night before to all of my media contacts with a complete schedule indicating where and when the candidate will be voting, where the candidate will be during the day, and the location of the Election Night party.

☐ I will send email reminders to all voter contacts to remind them to vote and invite them to the Election Night party.

☐ I may be the one lead staffer who stays in the office today, especially if there is a phone bank.

☐ If no presence in the office is necessary, I can work at a precinct.

☐ The media should be within easy reach and be able to speak with me all day.

☐ I will have a fully charged cell phone.

The Election Night Party

☐ All friends, family, contributors, volunteers, and supporters will be invited to a party to begin after the polls close.

☐ It is recommended that I reserve a room at a popular bar or restaurant.

☐ I may decide to have a party together with other minor party and Independent candidates. This is an especially good idea if multiple candidates are running locally. This increases my chances of media attention. I will be sure to thank everyone for their great work.

After the Campaign

Many first-time candidates neglect to properly finish their campaign business. This is a mistake that can lead to indebtedness and fines.

☐ I will meet with the campaign manager and key staff.

☐ I will determine what bills are outstanding and need to be paid.

☐ If I rented an office or equipment, or began telephone, cable, or Internet service for the campaign, I will need to end my contracts and service. I will take special care to be sure I am up to date and will no longer be charged.

☐ All bills and employees must be paid before I close my account.

☐ I will carefully keep track of every item in the office and place it in storage or return it to the proper owner. Campaigns often have problems with theft in the last days as volunteers sometimes feel "entitled."

☐ I will speak with my treasurer, finance director, and the Elections Office to determine what needs to be done with my campaign's bank account and finances. If I am planning to run for office in the future, I may be able to keep the campaign active.

☐ Some public officials decide to keep their campaigns open permanently so they can accept contributions at any time for the next race.

☐ I will remember that a legally active campaign usually requires reports to be filed by certain deadlines throughout the year, even if there hasn't been any activity.

☐ If I want to end the campaign completely, I will find out all legal responsibilities from the local Elections Office. I will ask about my options for any extra money in my account, or what to do in case of outstanding debts.

☐ I will take down all signage before the local deadline and as soon as possible. My neighbors will be thankful that I have taken care of my signs, and I will avoid any possible fines. Some types of signs and sign posts are re-usable. I will save these for my next campaign or donate them to someone else.

☐ I will gather up all my campaign material, literature, and promotional items. Certain things aren't worth keeping and should be thrown out, but I will keep some samples of each campaign item for future reference. I will save anything that might be useful in the future or serve as mementos for family and friends.

A Win-Win Situation

☐ I have found and organized a wonderful team of volunteers who love and respect me.

☐ I have found financial contributors who believe in me and can make things happen.

☐ The members of my community know that I care about them and that I am a valuable resource if they ever need my help.

☐ I have served my country, state, and locality with my dedication to a noble cause.

☐ Now, I have the opportunity to use all these new resources to continue the fight. The only way that I can lose is if I give up and quit after all this hard work and struggle.

NOTES:

NOTES:

18 Steps to Win a Local Election

Step 18:

Govern Well

"Freedom is a fragile thing and is never more than one generation away from extinction. It is not ours by inheritance; it must be fought for and defended constantly by each generation."

- Ronald Reagan

To govern well, an elected official must carefully weigh each vote. Advocates will often have well-reasoned arguments to support any proposal, so it is the official's job to ask the difficult questions. It is easy to just go along with the other elected officials on your board or approve everything your staff approves. Good people are elected to office every year. They become corrupt slowly. Expediency is the usual reason for giving away cherished principles. One decision, one vote at a time, good people become corrupt when they believe they can achieve good things by casting bad votes. Remember that abstaining from a controversial vote can be compared to a lie of omission.

Some proposals are complicated and offer a mixed bag of good and bad effects. There are many public policy groups that can help you sort through proposals that come before you. Reach out to the State Policy Network, your local political allies, and other independent think tanks for help.

How should I vote?

☐ Is this proposal the proper role for government?

☐ Is the proposal constitutional? (Federal, state, and local constitutions and charters apply.)

☐ Is this proposal legal?

☐ Will this proposal favor a select few at the expense of many?

☐ Have non-governmental solutions provided by private business, non-profits, charities, churches, or civic groups been properly considered before government action?

☐ What are the intended consequences of this proposal?

☐ Will there be unintended consequences?

☐ How much will this proposal cost? Is the cost less than the benefit?

☐ Are the proposed benefits real and measurable?

☐ Are there alternatives?

☐ Is this proposal moral and ethical?

☐ Does this proposal justify the expense of taxpayer dollars (and the coercion involved in tax collection)?

☐ Does this proposal violate any of my campaign promises or the intent of the people who voted for me?